THE OPEN UNIVERSITY
Arts: A Second Level Course
The Religious Quest

Unit 3
THE MAKING OF EARLY HINDUISM

Unit 4
CLASSICAL HINDU PHILOSOPHY AND THEOLOGY

The Open University Press

When you see the symbol in the right-hand margin turn to the Study Guide to *Worlds of Faith*.

The Open University Press
Walton Hall, Milton Keynes
MK7 6AA

First published 1987

Designed by the Graphic Design Group of the Open University.

Produced in Great Britain by Speedlith Photo Litho Ltd., Longford Trading Estate, Thomas Street, Stretford. M32 0JT

ISBN 0 335 11307 9

This text forms part of an Open University course. The complete list of units in the course appears at the end of this text.

For general availability of supporting material referred to in this text, please write to Open University Educational Enterprises Limited, 12 Cofferidge Close, Stony Stratford, Milton Keynes, MK11 1BY, Great Britain.

Further information on Open University courses may be obtained from the Admissions Office, The Open University, PO Box 48, Walton Hall, Milton Keynes, MK7 6AB.

1.1

Unit 3

THE MAKING OF EARLY HINDUISM

Written by Ninian Smart for the Course Team

Contents

1 Characteristics of classical Hinduism

1.1 Hinduism or Hinduisms?

India's religious history has been complex and rich. It was out of a number of early quests for salvation or liberation that some major religious traditions—Buddhism, Jainism and Hinduism—crystallized. Hinduism has turned out to be the dominant way of life in modern India, and you have already seen the persistent problem, namely how to define such a variegated religion at all. (Refer again to the discussion of the definition and diversity of Hinduism in Unit 1B, §1.1.)

1.1.1 Consider the following points:

(a) There are some Hindus who do not believe in God, yet are genuine Hindus. But most Hindus believe in God in some form or other.

(b) Most Hindus believe in rebirth or reincarnation, but it is not an article of any creed.

(c) Some Hindus worship Śiva, others Vishṇu, some both and some neither.

(d) Some Hindus are strict vegetarians; most are not.

And so we might go on.

Still, there are some prevailing characteristics which Hinduism came to acquire. I shall come to these in a moment.

1.1.2 Meanwhile, let us remember that after all the very term Hinduism is a modern one, derived in part from a term used by Muslims to designate the inhabitants of the lands on and beyond the Indus, namely Hindustan, and in part from the pervasive Western -ism. This categorization of things as '-isms' can be misleading, for it suggests a systematization of thought into a coherent whole which may not be the most important feature or may not even be a feature of the human phenomena in question.

1.1.3 You have seen from your reading of the article by A. L. Basham in the set book *The Concise Encyclopedia of Living Faiths*[1] pages 217–254 and from Units 1B–2, that there is no single creed or ideology in Hinduism. Rather it is a federation of cults and customs, a collage of ideas and spiritual aspirations. So in a way it would be better to speak of Hinduisms. However it has become too commonplace to speak of Hinduism for us to turn back the linguistic clock. Yet we should be on our guard. Isn't it too easy to think of religions as monolithic wholes, with internal variations? Consider this question further and write your own brief comment on it, referring to any religion you may be familiar with.

1.1.4 *An answer:* Even with Christianity, if you ask people 'what is Christianity?' you get a wide variety of replies; for some it is little more than doing good to one's neighbour; for others it involves acceptance of the authority of the Pope and of the central importance of the sacraments of the

[1] Zaehner, R. C. (ed) (1988) *The Hutchinson Encyclopedia of Living Faiths*, Rev. edn., Century Hutchinson, London (set book) hereafter cited as *Encyclopedia*.

Catholic Church; for others, it centres on belief in the Bible and the experience of personal conversion to Christ, and so on. A Romanian monastic church does not bear much resemblance to a Baptist chapel in Wigan, nor does a Friends' Meeting House resemble an Ethiopian cathedral. So it may be a facile assumption that there is a single thing called Christianity. What we can say is that there is a variety of forms of religion which can be traced back historically to the early Church. Things are even more complex with Hinduism because it did not even have a single founder, but rather has grown together into a loosely knit federation of Hinduisms. So behind each singular word we should perceive the plural.

1.2 Brāhmaṇs and class

Still, despite the problems of definition, as you have seen, there are some typical features of Hinduism. One of these is the general acceptance of the prestige and spiritual leadership of the Brāhmaṇ class. The Brāhmaṇs have hereditary rights as priests and custodians of the sacred scriptural tradition. Only a minority actually perform priestly functions, it is true; but the principle of the superiority of the Brāhmaṇ remains important. I have referred here to the Brāhmaṇ class—the word is used to translate the Sanskrit term *varṇa*, literally 'colour'. You have already studied the class-cum-caste system (Units 1B–2, §§2.3.2–2.3.4) and you will remember that Indian society was divided into three, then four and finally in effect five classes. Usually the number of varṇas recognized is four. The fifth class consists of the untouchables or harijans as Mahatma Gandhi dubbed them (the word means 'sons of Hari', that is to say sons or offspring of God).

1.2.1 The upper three classes are termed dvija or twice-born. The epithet is also used for birds: the first birth of a bird is when the egg is laid, the second when the chick comes out of the egg. The first birth of an upper-class Hindu is when he is born, and the second when he is endowed with the sacred thread he wears on his torso; that is, his second birth is when he is initiated into adult society. Originally only the upper three varṇas had access to the sacred scriptural tradition. Remember, however, that in using the term 'class' we are not referring to economic classes. A Brāhmaṇ could be a Harrovian like Nehru or a cook. An untouchable can be a millionaire, or a sweeper. You should refer again to the discussion of these and related matters in Units 1B–2, §§2.3.0–2.3.6.

1.2.2 In classical Hinduism, taking shape in the centuries just before and after the birth of Christ, the class system further proliferated into the *jāti* or caste system. As you have seen one does not marry outside one's caste nor eat with members of another caste. Didn't the British therefore become something of a caste when they ruled India?

An answer: When the British began bringing women to India, married to officers, administrators and so on, it became rather unusual for a British person to marry an Indian woman. The English club became an exclusively white preserve, and so in general most of the Englishman's eating and drinking was in the company of other Englishmen. Thus the British did develop into something very like an Indian caste. This was reinforced by the Indian caste system itself, which tended to discourage racial intermarriage.

1.3 The authority of śruti

So far, we have noted two features of classical Hinduism: the authority of the Brāhmaṇs and the class-cum-caste system. The former was important from the point of view of the transmission of sacred truths. For convenience I will call them scriptures, though originally they were handed down orally. The most sacred of these scriptures are the *Veda*, consisting of four divisions, typically, hymns or verses (the so called Vedic hymns), further portions known as *Brāhmaṇas* and *Āranyakas*; and those meditative and theological treatises known as *Upanishads*, which is the Anglicized form we use here for the Sanskrit Upaniṣads. These writings collectively are known as *śruti* or 'what is heard' (i.e. revelation as 'heard' by the seers of old). So a third feature of Hinduism is acceptance of the authority of śruti. The religious groups in ancient India who accepted the Vedic revelation were deemed *āstika* or orthodox, and those, like the Jains and Buddhists, who did not were termed *nāstika* or unorthodox. You will find the subject of the nature and authority of the Hindu scriptures dealt with in *Encyclopedia*, pages 218–220.

1.4 Different forms of God

A feature that came to pervade classical Hinduism was the cult of images, so that India became a land dense with temples. The original Aryan religion of the Vedic hymns developed amongst nomads, and at least partly for this reason there were no images, Vedic rites being performed in sacred spaces or under temporary shelters. The cult of images developed during the period of the great Epics, and brought with it a proliferation of the different forms of God. (For further information on the great Epics, see *Encyclopedia*, pp. 238 ff.) However, the gods came to be associated with, in the main, one of the two great traditions of worship, one directed to Śiva the other to Vishṇu. These two great gods were conceived as alternative manifestations of the one Reality, and are often also associated with *Brahmā* (the personal God of the Brāhmaṇs), in a sacred triad. But Brahmā is not much worshipped in separate form, so another typical characteristic of classical Hinduism is the cult of images and the worship of God.

1.5 Rebirth, karma and moksha

Lastly, one can single out an item of belief which pervades the Hindu world, indeed virtually the whole world of the Indian religions including Jainism, Buddhism and Sikhism, and that is belief in rebirth, reincarnation, metempsychosis or transmigration (different terms have been used in the West: in the ensuing I shall stick to 'rebirth' as the least loaded of the terms). As the idea developed, it was associated with the notion of *karma*, that is to say the law by which one's deeds determine one's future status in another life. Generally speaking, the Indian systems incorporate belief in a virtual infinity of previous lives, which could be in various forms, as men, animals, insects, ghosts, gods, in various grades of heaven or in punishing purgatories. Thus *moksha* or liberation was thought of as involving the cessation of the round of rebirth, in which the soul finally transcends the world and comes to peaceful rest, either by itself in blissful isolation or in communion with God. Against this framework of classical Hinduism, then, Indians have acted out the drama of life and the ultimate pursuit of moksha. (For a modern interpretation of moksha, read the article by K. Sivaraman in the *Reader*[1], §§2.7.1–2.7.4 'The meaning of moksha in contemporary Hindu thought and life'.)

1.6 Three exercises to recap

(a) Write a revisionary paragraph on the varṇa system, and enumerate the four classes. For this refer back to Simon Weightman's treatment of the question in Units 1B–2, §§2.3.2–2.3.4, and also to *Encyclopedia*, p. 244

(b) Now write brief notes on the following: moksha, Veda, Vedānta, Sanskrit, Aryan. (You will find relevant material in *Encyclopedia*, pp. 218–223 and 250–253.

(c) In order to clarify the differences and avoid confusion give the meanings of the following terms: Brahman, Brahmā, Brāhmaṇ and Brāhmaṇas. (Check in the Glossary.)

PLEASE PAUSE HERE

DO NOT READ ON UNTIL YOU HAVE COMPLETED THE EXERCISE

Specimen answer

(a) The varṇa system theoretically classifies Indians into four classes. These are, in order of precedence, the Brāhmaṇs who historically wielded priestly functions; the *kshatriyas* the warrior or noble class; the *vaiśyas,* who historically were cultivators and artisans. These top three classes, belonging to the original three-fold division of Aryan, and more generally Indo-European society, count as the dvija or twice-born. In principle the sacred lore of the Vedas was available only to these three classes. Below them came a fourth class, the *sūdras*, or labourers, who had limited rights and who seem to represent elements from the population conquered during the Aryan invasions of India. Below the four varṇas, there exists a fifth, *pañchama*, class, the untouchables. These often are involved in occupations which are ritually dirty; such as tanning (for skinning cows is sinful), fishing, sanitation, butchering, etc. Also belonging to this category are many of the tribal people still not fully absorbed into the fabric of orthodox Hindu society. You will recall that the varṇa system is not by itself the full caste system, which is more elaborate, but it provides a broad framework for it. Also, people do not necessarily have occupations corresponding to their historic functions.

(b) *Moksha* is one of the terms used for salvation or liberation in India. A word which is also sometimes used is *mukti*, which comes from the same root, of a verb meaning 'to free'. Typically moksha is seen as liberation from the round of rebirth. The means vary according to different schools of thought, and what moksha is conceived to be also varies.

Veda: literally this means knowledge or what is known. It is the term applied to the revealed tradition of orthodox Hinduism, and applies to four collections of hymns, the *Ṛig, Sāma, Yajur* and *Atharva* Vedas, together with further works known as Brāhmaṇas, Āranyakas and Upanishads.

[1] Foy, W. (ed) (1977) *Man's Religious Quest: A Reader*, Croom-Helm, London (course reader) hereafter cited as *Reader*.

Figure 1 Vishṇu in the centre of his ten avatārs; painting from Jaipur, India, eighteenth century. (Crown copyright, Victoria and Albert Museum.)

Read 218–223 ✓
" 250–258

Vedānta: the end of the Veda, a term used to signify those systems of Hindu theology (or philosophy) which systematize the teaching about ultimate Reality as found in the Upanishads. The best known of the systems of Vedānta are: Non-dualism (*Advaita Vedānta*), whose chief exponent was *Śaṅkara*, Qualified Non-dualism (*Viśishtādvaita*), whose chief exponent was *Rāmānuja*, and Dualism (*Dvaita*), whose chief exponent was *Madhva* (see Unit 4, §4). These systems take their names from the relationship posited in each between God and the soul: for Śaṅkara they are identical, for example.

Sanskrit: the language of classical India, an early form of which is used in the Vedic hymns. It is related to Greek and Latin, and was the forerunner of the vernacular languages of northern India, such as Hindi and Gujarati.

Aryan: an English term derived from the Sanskrit *ārya,* which literally means 'noble' and which was applied by the Vedic Indians to their own tradition and community. The Aryan invaders of India spoke an Indo-European language related to ancient Latin and Greek, and may have originated in the Baltic area or in the southern steppes.

(c) *Brahman:* the 'holy power', Ultimate Reality (see §§3.1.1 and 3.5.6 below).

Brahmā: 'the personal God of the Brāhmaṇs' (see §1.4 above).

Brāhmaṇ: the highest varṇa in the class hierarchy (see §1.2 above).

Brāhmaṇas: one portion of the scriptures or *śruti* (see §1.3 above).

2 Problems of textual study

2.1 Original meaning, interpretation and comparison

In this unit I shall be examining some passages from two major texts from ancient India, namely the *Īśā Upanishad* and the *Bhagavad-Gītā*. (You will find references to both these works in *Encyclopedia*, pp. 230–233. For the text of the passages refer to *Reader*, §§2.5 'The Īśā Upanishad and the Khandogya Upanishad' and 2.6 'The Bhagavad-Gītā.'

2.1.1 But it is unwise to think that you can simply study a religion by reading its scriptures, though this is a common fallacy. The reasons why such an approach is unsatisfactory are various. First, you need to know how the scriptures are actually used, and this may not be evident from their contents. Thus you cannot tell from reading the Gospels that they are read out at the Anglican Eucharist or at the Roman Catholic Mass. And until you know how they are, and have been, used you will not know how important they are for determining the spiritual life of the tradition in question. Second, in order to understand the scriptures it will be necessary to know something about forms of religious life and practice, for example, what yoga or worship is like. Third, there may be much non-scriptural evidence which is important for getting a rounded picture of the historical setting of a religion. Also you need to ask yourself what you are doing in exploring a scripture. Are you trying to elicit the ideas from it which you believe to be valid? That is, are we using it as a basis for some kind of theology or expression of our own convictions? Are you simply trying to bring out what the scripture meant to those who composed it and used it? Are you using the scriptures as so much historical evidence? Are we trying to bring out what the scripture meant to the modern adherent of the faith? Clearly, these differing enterprises need not be incompatible, and some necessarily overlap. But I think we should all be clear in our own mind what we are doing.

2.1.2 I shall try to adopt the following approach. First, I shall try to elicit the original meaning of the text. Second, I shall refer to some ways in which it has been interpreted according to the Hindu tradition. Third, I shall comment on comparisons which can be made with aspects of religion beyond the Hindu tradition. I think it is worth making comparisons explicitly, because we often approach another religion with assumptions about the nature of religion derived from our own culture, assumptions which need not always, or at all, apply to another tradition. Let me illustrate this last point by considering the Hindu attitude to the many gods as it emerged in the Vedic hymns and later. For the Westerner does not know quite how to cope with this attitude: it looks like polytheism, but it also has a ring of monotheism about it (for these are two key categories fashioned in the experience of the classical and Christian West).

2.2 Trans-polytheistic theism

In the Ṛig Veda there is a famous verse which reads as follows:

> They call it Indra, Mitra, Varuṇa and Agnī
> And also heavenly delightful Garutman:
> The Real is one, though sages name it variously.

In other words, the different gods are reflections of one reality.

Question

Write brief notes on the important gods Indra, Agnī, Mitra, Varuṇa. (Refer here to *Encyclopedia*, pp. 218–221, and 228.

PLEASE PAUSE HERE

DO NOT READ ON UNTIL YOU HAVE COMPLETED THE EXERCISE

Specimen answer

Indra: the atmospheric stormy warrior deity of the Aryans, described in the Vedic hymns as helping the Aryans to conquer the peoples they encountered in north-west India (who doubtless included the inhabitants of the great Indus Valley civilization cities, which came to be abandoned in the second millennium BC, probably because of the action of the waves of

Figure 2 Indra, King of the Gods making a gesture of explanation. (Nepal Museum, Katmandu. Photoatelier: H. Thiele and H. Munker.)

Figure 3 Agnī, the God of Fire, Khajuraho, Chandella dynasty, eleventh century CE. *(Bury Peerless.)*

invaders). Indra declined in importance in later times, though he appears as Sakka, an important god in the Buddhist Pali canon.

Agnī: the fire god, associated above all with the sacred fire used in Vedic sacrificial ritual. Fire has three forms—the sun, lightning and earthly fire, so Agnī operates at various levels of reality, and through his sacrificial role he is importantly mediator between gods and men.

Mitra: a version of the sun-god, especially significant because he is the same as Mithra, the Iranian deity important in Zoroastrianism and the central figure of the religion of Mithraism which spread through the legions of the Roman empire.

Varuṇa: for a period possibly the most important god of the Vedic pantheon. His name relates to the Greek Ouranos and Latin Uranus (i.e. Heaven). As sky-god Varuṇa was upholder of cosmic order, including human morality. His supremacy faded with the rise of the great gods Vishṇu and Śiva.

3 The Īśā-Upanishad

Let us now proceed to contemplate our first major text, namely the Īśā Upanishad, of which I shall offer an English translation, verse by verse, and a commentary on some of the salient points. This will give us a series of 'pegs' on which we can hang our discussion of some of the main questions which concern you in this course. My commentary, of course, is inevitably one choice out of possible alternatives. Before you begin your study of the Īśā Upanishad you should look at *Reader*, §2.5 and *Encyclopedia*, pp. 218 ff again.

3.1 Verse 1

> All this, whatever moves in the moving cosmos, is enveloped by the Lord (*īśā*). So be content with what is granted [alternatively: 'Enjoy yourself through renunciation']: do not covet the belongings of others.

3.1.1 The Upanishad is named after its first two syllables, the term Īśā which is another version of the term *Īśvara* or Lord, commonly used in the later period for God considered as personal Being and Creator. The other key expression in the Upanishads is *Brahman*, the 'holy power'. This is used to refer to ultimate Reality, which may or not be personally conceived. Indeed Brahman is a neuter word, originally meaning the power implicit in the sacrificial ritual, and so the power wielded by Brāhmaṇs. Once the whole cosmos was thought of as a sacrificial ritual, the power sustaining it was considered to be Brahman (see the explanation in *Encyclopedia*, p. 219.

3.1.2 The idea that the cosmos is enveloped by the Lord points to the true meaning of life, namely living for God. As we shall see in the next verse, there is a special sense in which 'renunciation' is used, which links this Upanishad with the teachings of the Bhagavad-Gītā (qv). Sometimes the doctrine of the inclusion of the world within God is called panentheistic literally 'all-in-God-ism'. Of course, one cannot take the terms 'enveloped' or 'in' in quite a literal sense, for God transcends space, which is after all co-extensive with the world, as it is here conceived.

3.2 Verse 2

> Always here performing works one should desire to live a hundred years. Living as a man there is no other way whereby the deed does not adhere to you.

3.2.1 The word I have translated as 'works' is *karmāni*. It is the plural of karma, which appears near the end of the second verse, translated as 'deed'. This points to certain ambiguities in the term karma as used in the Indian tradition. First, it can simply mean deeds, actions or works. More particularly it can mean those works which are required of you, namely one's duties (as determined by one's varṇa or jāti, that is to say one's station in life, cf. §2.1 above). So far then it can be translated in the plural as 'acts' and as 'duties'. Third, however, karma can mean sacrificial or ritual acts, as performed by the priest in the course of Vedic ritual. It can be translated in this sense of the term as 'ritual acts', but the meaning which has received the most widespread attention is that in which karma refers to the state of affairs whereby a man's deed bears fruit (*karmaphala*). This fruit came to be interpreted against the background of belief in rebirth, so that not only do my acts have an effect on this life, but also in the next life (and the next life after that, etc). Likewise my present state in this life is in part determined by what I did in previous lives. So the fourth meaning is the 'Law of karma'. Different systems of Indian religion and philosophy have different theories of how karma operates. For Buddhism, it is primarily a psychological law (for an account of the Buddhist theory of karma see *Encyclopedia*, pp. 274–278). For Jainism (see *Encyclopedia*, pp. 255–262), karma is treated in a rather material way as though particles of karma accumulate in a soul and weigh it down, preventing it from rising to the summit of the universe, whither liberated souls ascend. For the theistic schools (see Unit 4) karma is seen as an expression of God's will in apportioning fates to different individuals.

3.2.2 The meaning of the verse as a whole is open to question, but the most natural interpretation is that those who live in the world and perform their religious and other duties should perform them in the spirit of verse 1 of the Īśā Upanishad, that is, by not wishing for any reward from them. In that case, the karmic effects will not cling to him. This is a theme which we shall come back to in the discussion of the Gītā.

3.2.3 For Śaṅkara—the chief exponent of non-dualism (you will meet him again in Unit 4, §2.1)—however, the verse implies a distinction between those who live in the world and the *sannyāsin* or recluse who leaves the world in order to attain perfect knowledge of the Self.

3.2.4 It is worth looking here at the ideal of the sannyāsin, as it was important in India in the period of the Upanishads (say 800–500 BC), and has remained important right through to the present time. (For information on the sannyāsin ideal in practice see Units 1B-2; §4.9.2 and *Encyclopedia*, p. 248 and p. 250.) The literature of the early period refers to 'brāhmaṇas and *śranaḥas*' as two kinds of holy men, the latter being wandering recluses. Some of these organized themselves into groups. Put on a formal basis these became the monastic orders of Buddhism and Jainism, and such orders in Hinduism as that of Śaûkara's own order and in modern times the *Rāmakṛishṇa* order. Recluses however could be hermits, and a class of brāhmaṇical hermits were known as the forestdwellers, who were an important group for the composition of the later Vedic texts, including the Upanishads.

3.2.5 Just to clarify the types of recluses to be found (not only in early India but in other religious traditions as well), we distinguish between those who are eremitical and those who are cenobitical (i.e. who live together), and between those who are based in monasteries and those who are not. Thus we can see the types in the following table.

Table 1

Types	Monastic	Non-monastic
eremitical		X
cenobitical (who live together)	X	X

3.2.6 Monastic living was a late development when groves and other pieces of land were granted to cenobitical groups, who came thus to settle on them and build. A further dimension to the ideal of the sannyāsin was ovided by the evolution within Hinduism of the concept of the four stages life (originally three) for the dvija. This was a means of controlling the movement to renounce the world, which had somewhat burgeoned through the success of Buddhism in recruiting young men and women into the *Sangha*. The four stages are conceived, then, as:

(i) Being a student, *brahmacarin* (the term implies that a young person at this stage is celibate).

(ii) Being a householder, *gṛhasta* (the term implies marriage and bringing up a family).

(iii) Beginning to shed family responsibilities as a *vānaprastha*, literally 'forest-dweller'.

(iv) Giving up the world utterly, as a wandering sannyāsin.

The third stage means that the householder now hands over responsibilities to the son, and begins to withdraw from worldly duties and concerns, possibly building himself a retreat near the household. In various modified forms the ideal still exists in modern India. (See *Encyclopedia*, pp. 240–243.)

3.3 Verse 3

> Diabolical, truly, are those spheres of existence covered in darkness, and to them after death go those people who kill the self.

The *asuras* (from which we get the adjective *asurya*) were the antigods of the Vedic hymns, against whom the Aryan gods struggled; and the verse suggests an evil fate for those who neglect the self. It is natural to identify this self with the eternal *ātman*, so literally it cannot be killed, a point made very forcibly in the Bhagavad-Gītā (see below, §4.5). But those who pursue worldly goods cover over the self with a layer of ignorance. I take the next two verses together.

3.4 Verses 4 and 5

> It is unmoving, one, faster than the mind. The senses do not reach it, for it is always one ahead. Though standing it outstrips the runner. In it the air supports the acts of beings.
>
> It moves and it moves not: it is far and it is near; it is within all this and also it is outside all this.

3.4.1 To my mind these are the most important and profound verses of this Upanishad and indeed contain the essence of much Upanishadic teaching. Of course, at this juncture we need to bear in mind that there are diverse interpretations of the Vedic scriptures, and they do not necessarily form a consistent whole, though traditional commentators, believing in their divine provenance, could scarcely do other than try to find in them a wholly consistent thought-structure. Later we shall look more systematically at two systems of interpretation, those of Saṇkara and Rāmānuja (Unit 4, §§2 and 3).

3.4.2 The first main point made in these verses is that it, which presumably is Brahman, outstrips the senses, even the mind or *manas*. In classical Indian philosophy manas meant the inner organ which coordinated the reports of the sense organs. Thus if I am looking at a pink flower, I not only see its colour but also its shape and recognize that it is soft and cool. manas.

In other words I put together into one object the various reports of the senses. This work of synthesis is, then, what the mind does. In brief Brahman is not an object of perception. Yet as we shall see it does not follow that there is no experience of Brahman.

3.4.3 Verse 4 also states that the divine being is somehow the framework within which the air supports the activities of beings. A more modern way of putting this would be to say that the acts of beings occur in space (for sometimes space, ether and air were identified in ancient Indian thought), which somehow is within God. In other words, the divine being is as it were behind all beings as their support. Turning now to verse 5, and in particular the statement that the divine reality is both far and near, we now see the two sides of the author's conception of Brahman. On the one hand, Brahman is far, being beyond the world as transcendent source of all things and within which beings operate. On the other hand, Brahman is totally near, for he is within the individual, as the self or *ātman*. If one can therefore penetrate to the self, presumably by the practice of meditation, whereby one goes beyond sense-perception or mental images, one reaches the Divine.

ātman (self)

3.5 Brahman and ātman

3.5.1 It is notable in these verses that the universe ('all this') is seen as a unity. This was already beginning to be apparent in the Vedic hymns, where Varuna presided over *ṛita* or cosmic order. Thus part of the Upanishadic discovery is not just the unity of the cosmos but the unity behind the unity.

3.5.2 However, where the verses state that Brahman both moves and does not, an ambiguity comes in. Because Brahman is the inner essence of the universe, sometimes the moving world of perception is also seen as Brahman (just as my essence is seen in my bodily behaviour even if my heart and soul lie beyond the visible manifestations). Consequently, the verses figure Brahman also as manifest universe, moving, even if behind there is a changeless being.

The main message seems to be the identification of soul and God, of Self and Brahman, however: and about this identification, so central to the Upanishads, there are questions. Let us pause here and ask a central one.

Question

3.5.3 Why should some of the authors of the Chāndogya Upanishad have identified Brahman and ātman? (For this exercise it will be relevant to read the passages from the Chāndogya Upanishad in the *Reader*, §2.5.11–2.5.26[1]. Refer also to *Encyclopedia*, pp. 220–221 and 230.)

PLEASE PAUSE HERE

DO NOT READ ON UNTIL YOU HAVE COMPLETED THE EXERCISE

[1] Further reading material on this subject is:
Smart, N. (1958) *Reasons and Faiths*, Routledge & Kegan Paul, London.
Zimmer, H. (1957) *Philosophies of India*, Dewer Books, London.
Renou, L. (1954) *Religions of Ancient India*, Athlone Press, London.

Specimen answer and discussion

3.5.4 The period when the Upanishads were composed was one of speculation among the Brāhmaṇs and others committed to the Vedic tradition about the meaning of sacrificial ritual. One line of thinking was to extrapolate out from sacrifice to the cosmos. In this way the holy power Brahman operative within the rites was also the power sustaining the whole universe. Thus we see the emergence of the conception of the holy Power lying behind everything. At the same time that power was also implicit in the *Brāhmin* class itself.

3.5.5 Meanwhile the śramaṇas or recluses (cf §3.2.4 above) who by their austerity and prestige attracted much support from the ordinary folk living in the now prospering Gangetic basin, offered some alternative theories. Their expertise was not priestly but psychological, in that they practised methods of meditation and self-mortification, reportedly giving them great powers—greater indeed often than those of the gods. Some of the śramanic religious movements developed into traditions now known as Jainism and Buddhism, and also into the *Ajīvikas* and others, once important but now no longer surviving (on the Ajīvikas, see *Encyclopedia*, p. 255). However, in the Upanishads we see a synthesis of ideas. Perchance the inner self revealed in mystical consciousness through the practice of yoga and austerity was that Brahman inherent in the Brāhmaṇ class and in the individual Brāhmaṇ. It could thus also be seen as identical with the Brahman 'out there', source of and sustainer of the whole moving cosmos. In this way a grand synthesis between ritual, yoga and cosmology was achieved.

3.5.6 It was also a likely theory from the following points of resemblance between ātman and Brahman. *Firstly*, Brahman was source of movement, itself unmoving; likewise within the person the self lay behind mind, breath and life, and was itself unaffected by the changes going on in the individual's life. *Second*, the Power behind the world was beyond seeing. What can be seen, felt, heard, smelt and so on is the *jagat*, the cosmos of moving beings. So also yoga involves going beyond perception or thoughts, and stilling the psyche until one achieves a pure imageless consciousness. *Third*, if rituals can have limited, but important effects, then the holy Power in the world must have supreme potency: but the ritual depends on the inner life and knowledge of the priest. So it is reasonable to see a correspondance between inner and outer powers, between the self (or selves) within conscious beings and the self within the world. *Fourth*, the priest's knowledge (and Veda means knowledge) is matched by the inner knowledge or mystical gnosis of the yogi—both are secret, and affect the world, either through rites or magic powers. This indeed is why in knowing the inner essence of the self one knows the nature of the whole world. Conversely Brahman as creator uses magic power to generate beings—in later Hinduism the figure of Śiva as the great yogi, the *Mahāyogi*, of great power, is a striking symbol of this conception. *Fifth*, at the social level, the ātman–Brahman equation could mean the coalescence of the two sources of magical charisma. Perhaps we can see a reflection of similar tendencies in the work of Radhakrishnan and other modern Hindu thinkers to absorb and mould ideas from outside their own system.

3.5.7 Also, it may be noted that mystics in other religions have sometimes made a similar equation. This is partly because somehow for them the experience seems to abolish the difference between the subject and the object, between soul and God. (Here you may usefully consider the references to mysticism in *Encyclopedia*, pp. 193–194 and 368–369.)

3.6 Brahman and creation

3.6.1 There is a question which particularly the Westerner might use to interrogate the Upanishads—how does Brahman create? If the universe is somehow dependent upon It or Him, then surely there must have been a time when he or it created the world? The readings give two accounts of creation—but we need to ask whether they mean events in time or not. If I say 'Carelessness breeds folly, and folly ignorance', do I mean that first a man is careless, then foolish, then stupid? Already the relationship should be seen to be more complex than that. So it could be that strange creation stories in the Upanishads do not necessarily speak of a point in time or at the beginning of time. They may have more to do with an exploration of the dependence of the cosmos on God, rather than its origin in some fiat.

3.6.2 For already by the time of the Upanishads non-orthodox ideas, and especially the Buddhist cosmology, were beginning to have a profound impact upon the Aryan tradition. And this cosmology saw no beginning to the universe, only great pulsating ages of collapse and renewal (see *Encyclopedia*, pp. 223–224). So creation was beginning to be perceived as a mode of relationship rather than as a single, primeval act. Roughly, therefore, the Hindu tradition tended to think of the world as everlasting, but created (continuously and recurrently) by God. In this the Hindus thought like the Arabian philosopher Averroes, the Jewish Maimonides (see *Encyclopedia*, pp. 22–23) and (to some extent) St Thomas Aquinas (but Aquinas thought that while reason did not disprove the possibility of an eternally created world, that possibility was excluded by *Genesis*, which he took fairly literally).

To some degree the creator in the Upanishads is referred to as a person. One question needing to be asked about the Īśā is how far Brahman can be considered a personal being. According to Basham (see *Encyclopedia*, p. 230[1]), verse 8 is significant in this direction, for the verse begins *sa*, the pronoun meaning 'he'. To this we shall briefly return, but now let us proceed to the intervening passages. I take 6 and 7 together.

3.7 Verses 6 and 7

> He then who sees all beings in his self, and his self in all beings, does not worry. When, to someone who *knows*, all beings have become one with his own self, what delusion or sorrow can occur to him: he has perceived the oneness.

A natural way to take the last part of these verses is that the oneness is not just the unique character, the oneness in this sense, of Brahman, but rather the identity between the cosmic self and the inner self. There can now be no question of folly or sorrow, for God or Brahman is beyond such weaknesses and disadvantages. Once again we note in the Indian tradition the coupling together of lack of insight (ignorance) and suffering. The same theme runs through Buddhism, for example (you will find this explained in Units 5–7). The problem is not sin, but folly; not alienation precisely, but ignorance; not lack of will-power but absence of vision—an important contrast of style between Christian and Indian thinking. By contrast knowledge brings

[1] See also Basham, A.L. (1975), *The Wonder that was India*, Fontana, London, p. 254.

liberation—not of course book-knowledge or an OU degree, but spiritual insight into the nature of the world and of the Transcendent. The person with such knowledge becomes one with God, perhaps identical (though here questions of interpretation enter in once again) but at any rate the insightful person is able at least to share some divine characteristics. And so we come to verse 8.

3.8 Verse 8

> He fills all, radiant, bodiless, unconquerable, sinewless, pure, devoid of evil. He is the seer and thinker, pervading all, self-existent, and has distributed through endless times tasks to beings in accordance with their character.

Here there seems to be an explicitly more personal view of God, who is also seen not only as outside karma and the vicissitudes of the world but as controller of what goes on in time. One of the epithets ascribed to the Lord here is *svāyaṁbhu* (self-existent) which is the Indian equivalent of the Western idea of God as necessary being (i.e. one whose existence does not depend on anything else's).

This is far enough to pursue the commentary of the Īśā. But it brings out some central preoccupations of the Upanishads. In the period after they were composed, great transformations occurred within the traditions destined to coalesce and to form classical Hinduism. However, the scriptural tradition of the Veda and Upanishads came to be projected right through Hindu history till the modern period as a source of doctrine and a normative revelation. Hence the question of the right interpretation of texts such as the Īśā remains vital for the self-understanding of the Brahmanical tradition.

4 The Bhagavad-Gītā

4.1 The prehistory of the Gītā

4.1.1 These features which we earlier identified as typifying classical Hinduism were in process of development in the period when the Bhagavad-Gītā itself was being formed. (Refer to *Encyclopedia*, pp. 246–247.) As we shall see, the poem is complex, and it is reasonable to infer that it had a complex prehistory. For one thing it came to be composed within the tradition of the cult of Kṛishṇa and Vishṇu. Let us pause to contemplate this strand in Indian religious history.

4.1.2 It is clear to anyone visiting contemporary India that devotional religion, namely the fervent worship of God, is central, one might say crucial, to the religiosity of most ordinary Hindus. This is not to deny that gurus and yogis, holy men of various kinds, in a word sannyāsins, (see §3.2.6 above) are also vital, nor to deny that the life of inner contemplation is regarded widely as most important. Still, the *bhakti* or devotion accorded to great manifestations of God such as Vishṇu is also inescapably evident in the framework of Hindu piety. It breathes through temples, through modes of dress, through posters and literature, through all kinds of expressions in everyday life.

4.1.3 It would seem that the cult of Vishṇu, though ancient, was perhaps first most prominent in the devotion accorded to one of his *avatars* or incarnations, Kṛishṇa. This dark-blue God of north India, whose main exploits occurred in Vrindaban, not far from Agra, is the hidden hero of the Gītā. With *Rāma* he is the most vital incarnation of Vishṇu, for between them they divide the two great Epics, the *Mahābhārata* and the *Rāmāyana*. These two epics have had wide circulation and influence throughout India, and serve both as vehicles of entertainment and of religious and moral instruction. Incorporated into the Mahābhārata is the poem usually known as the Bhagavad-Gītā or 'song of the Lord'. Its date of composition is open to question, but perhaps it reached its present form about 100 BC—though Hindu tradition ascribes it to the legendary ancient sage Vyāsa. Because of its powerful spiritual message (or messages, for different strands of thinking are woven into the work), it has gained immense influence, and has the status of being a subordinate scripture.

4.1.4 The Vedic writings down to the Upanishads are known as śruti or revelation (see, §1.3 above). The term literally means 'what is heard', the view being that the *ṛishis* or ancient holy men, heard the revelations contained in the everlasting Veda. But other works, notably the Laws of Manu (see further, *Encyclopedia*, p. 222) which define classical Hindu religions and social laws, and the Gītā are considered as *smṛiti*—literally 'what is remembered'. Such works are accorded the status of being subsidiary scriptures. In the south, among the Tamils, other works called *āgamas* were accorded authoritative status; so regarding scriptural matters the Indian scene is complex. However, whatever the technical status of the *Gītā*, it is probably the best-loved and most effective piece of Indian religious writing. In particular it and the Gospels profoundly affected the thoughts and attitudes of Mahatma Gandhi.

(what is heard)
śruti
(revelation)

smriti -
what is remembered

4.1.5 The elements which enter into the thought of the Gītā are: first, the bhakti cult devoted to Kṛishṇa; second, the related systems known as *Sāṇkhya* and *Yoga;* and third, some Buddhist and other ideas (see further

(a)

(b)

(c)

(d)

Figure 4 (a)–(h). The Kṛishṇa legend. Two of the most prominent figures of popular Hinduism over the centuries, figures appearing also in many Hindu philosophical treatises, are Kṛishṇa and Rāma. (a)–(h) illustrate some of the main episodes in the myth of Kṛishṇa (for Rāma see Fig. 7). Kṛishṇa is the eighth avatār of Vishṇu and appeared on earth to overthrow the demon Kamsa. Kṛishṇa's life is important not only for his overthrow of Kamsa, but also because he characterizes the ideal for so many ages; the cuddly baby, the mischievous youth, the ardent lover and the noble warrior. (a) shows a scene from the birth stories of Kṛishṇa. His father carries the baby Kṛishṇa away from the imprisonment in the palace of the evil Kamsa. Father and son are protected in their passage across the raging Jumna river by the serpent Shesha. (b) shows Kṛishṇa as the mischievous child being scolded for stealing the curds. As baby and child Kṛishṇa is the object of much popular motherly devotion. In (c) and (d) Kṛishṇa appears as the ardent lover; the seducer of milkmaids said to symbolize the active search by God for the love of the soul. In (c) Kṛishṇa hides the saris of the milkmaids in the tree and will only return them if the milkmaids stop hiding themselves and ask openly for their dearest wish. In (d) Kṛishṇa seduces his favourite milkmaid, Rādha (in which episode is seen the great example of the divine quest for the human soul).

(g)

(h)

(e)–(h) illustrate the theme of the heroic Kṛishṇa. In (e) Kṛishṇa has plunged into the waters to overpower the serpent which had been poisoning the waters with its venom. In (f) Kṛishṇa holds a mountain on his finger to shelter the village of Vrindaban from a storm sent by the Vedic god Indra, thus illustrating his superiority over the old gods. In (g) Kṛishṇa achieves the immediate purpose of his incarnation, the toppling of the wicked Kamsa from his throne and his death. (h) shows the great warrior. Arjuna, in his moment of doubt at the battle of Kurukshetra, the setting for the Bhagavad-Gītā, *perhaps the most popular of all Hindu religious writings. (Photos a, b, by kind permission of Chandigarh Museum; c, g, by kind permission of National Museum, Delhi; d, e, f, by kind permission of Baroda Museum; photos by Bury Peerless.)*

Encyclopedia, pp. 225–226). 'As for the story of Kṛishṇa, many Hindus regard it as literal history; and it may well be that there was a historical figure around when the myth was built. Thus in the Chāndogya Upanishad (III.17.6, *Reader*, §2.5.11) there is a reference to Kṛishṇa son of Devakī, who was a pupil of Ghora Angirasa, who taught that a person is indestructible, immovable and breath (or life itself)—teachings which are indeed reflected in the Gītā. Kṛishṇa was supposed to have been born as a prince of the Yadava people of the region of Mathura; and the legends about him include many tales of his miraculous and prankish childhood. But threatened by the evil Kamsa, he went to live with cowherds in the region of Vrindaban. Stories of his love affairs with the *gopis* or cowmaidens serve as images of the love between God and human souls. Then, as in the Gītā, Kṛishṇa emerges as a heroic warrior and friend of Arjuna, whom he helps in the great battles of the civil war described in the Mahābhārata.

4.1.6 The elements of Sāṇkhya in the Gītā are somewhat important. They are not used in quite the way they occur in the philosophical system known as Sāṇkhya, but it is worth outlining the structure of the latter and its place within the general scheme of Indian thought.

4.2 The six āstika schools

4.2.1 Traditionally Indian philosophy has been divided into those schools which accept the Veda as authoritative and those which do not (see §1.3 above). They are referred to respectively as āstika and nāstika schools. The latter include Buddhist schools, Jainism, anti-religious materialists and so on. The six orthodox (āstika) schools have become fitted into a scheme which, though it is not altogether logical, is usually used by Indian philosophical writers. The six come in related pairs and are as follows:

(i) Nyāya (Logic)
and
Vaiśeshika (Atomism)

(ii) Sāṇkhya (Distinctionism)
and
Yoga

(iii) Mīmāmsā (Exegesis)
and
Vedānta

4.2.2 I have put my own translations in parenthesis but you may prefer to use those of Basham (*Encyclopedia*, pp. 231–233). In the case of Yoga and Vedānta, since these terms are now current in English, a formal translation is superfluous but I shall in due course comment on the meanings of these terms. However, Vedānta will mainly be discussed in Unit 4, since the interpretation and systematization of the Vedic doctrines, which is the chief task of Vedānta, has given rise to important and conflicting schools, whose disputes are more important than any others for the understanding of Indian religions and philosophical ideas. This is one reason why the six-fold classification is somewhat artificial: somewhat like dividing fruit into apples, oranges and other fruits, when the differences between the others may be much more vital than the differences between apples and oranges.

Question

4.2.3 Write brief notes on the main concerns of the six different schools (basing your answer on *Encyclopedia*, pp. 231–233).

PLEASE PAUSE HERE

DO NOT READ ON UNTIL YOU HAVE COMPLETED THE EXERCISE

Specimen answer

(i) *Nyāya:* has mainly to do with the analysis of logical and other arguments used in reasoning and induction.

(ii) *Vaiśeshika:* a theory in which the elements are analysed into atoms. In so far as it has a religious message it is that the soul should be disentangled from matter.

(iii) *Sāṇkhya:* a dualistic metaphysics, essentially atheistic, according to which innumerable souls (*purushas*) are entangled in nature (*prakṛiti*). The aim is to gain insight into the essential difference between soul and matter, and so gain release from the latter.

(iv) *Yoga:* a system of practical contemplation, predicated on *Sāṇkhya* metaphysical assumptions.

(v) *Mīmāmsā:* a system of exegesis of Vedic texts, mainly concentrating on the practical implications of the texts in terms of ritual, etc.

(vi) *Vedānta:* an organized system of expounding the disjointed doctrines of the Upanishads, concentrating on salvation according to the Vedic rules and the belief in release through knowledge of the unity of brahman and ātman.

4.3 Sāṇkhya and Yoga

4.3.1 Sāṇkhya (sometimes transliterated *Sāmkhyā*) needs further explanation. The souls which are implicated in nature are in process of rebirth until a person achieves liberation, and most typically the practice of yoga is seen as the means to attaining it, for yoga purifies the consciousness in such a way that the true nature of the purusha becomes evident, and its essential otherness from prakṛiti. This experience brings about *viveka* or discrimination, and thus the person will not be reborn and will be freed from the suffering (*dukhha*) which characterizes the life of living beings in the round of rebirth. Hence the Yoga system, which sets forth one main pattern of meditation, is seen in close conjunction with Sāṇkhya. (See also Basham's account in *Encyclopedia*, pp. 231–233.) Here we need to pause to consider the multiple meanings of the term yoga.

4.3.2 I shall here adopt the following convention, of spelling Yoga with a capital Y when referring to the system known as Yoga, which is, one of the six schools. But yoga with a small y I shall use to refer to the whole set of methods of meditation and self-control found in the Indian (including the Buddhist and Jain) tradition. The term seems to be cognate with our word 'yoke', and implies harnessing one's mental powers in order to concentrate. Much of yoga is similar to the mystical practice of other traditions, such as in Sufism and Christian contemplation. Indeed recently there has been some attempt by Christians to use Indian techniques and thus to evolve a Christian yoga. In brief, to be a yogi one needs to practice yoga, but need not necessarily subscribe to the theory (roughly Sāṇkhya) and practise as described in the Yoga school.

4.3.3 However, to complicate matters the Gītā uses the term yoga in a very wide sense, rather idiosyncractically, to mean discipline or practice in general, as when it refers for instance to bhakti yoga or the discipline of devotion. Thus to follow what the Gītā means by bhakti yoga you do not need to be a yogi, still less to believe Yoga. Let us then set out the various terms and meanings:

Yoga: a school.
yoga: methods of self-control and meditation.
bhakti yoga: the practice of devotion. (Also referred to as *bhakti mārga.*)
yogi: a practitioner of yoga.
yoginī: a woman practitioner of yoga.
mahāyogi: the great yogi, epithet of Śiva.

The main form of mental discipline has come to be called *rāja-yoga* or royal yoga. A late development has been the elaboration of a form of bodily gynmanstics or physical yoga known as *haṭha-yoga.*

4.3.4 The school Yoga relies, as has been noted, on Sāṇkhya for its metaphysical framework. But while Sāṇkhya is atheistic, Yoga did develop belief in a God: the Lord is not creator, but the one soul never to have become entangled in the material world and the round of *saṁsāra.* As such he is a suitable object of meditation and can in this way help the yogi to achieve liberation (which does not however consist in union with God but rather in a kind of glorious isolation in which the soul experienced no more pain. On the doctrine of saṁsāra see further *Encyclopedia*, pp. 217 and 221.)

4.3.5 An aspect of Sāṇkhya of great importance for the Gītā, and for Indian cosmology generally, was its theory of evolution through the interplay of three forces known as the *guṇas,* literally 'qualities'. According to the picture of the universe which came to predominate in the Indian tradition, it 'pulsates' over long ages, known as *kalpas,* and alternates between a state of repose and a state of evolution and ultimate collapse, when a new age of respose occurs—and so on indefinitely. Each kalpa lasts 42,000 million years. The Sāṇkhya theory explains how from a state of repose the evolution of a formed state of the universe occurs. During a period of repose, souls are quiescent, their karma latent; while nature is a more or less featureless blend of the three guṇas. The latter are: *sattva, rajas* and *tamas,* which can be roughly translated as 'brightness', 'energy' and 'denseness'. These three forces correspond also to psychological types (you will find further explanation in *Encyclopedia*, p. 232). A person with much sattva has a clear and nimble intellect; one with much rajas is passionate and energetic; and one with much tamas is dull, dense. It is an entertaining pastime assigning proportions of the three guṇas to one's friends.

gunas
sattva – brightness (virtue)
rajas – energy (passion)
tamas – denseness (dullness)

4.3.6 The fact that in Sāṇkhya the guṇas are both psychological and material forces may be surprising to the Westerner (for in the West the difference between mind and body is taken rather seriously). But it is natural in the Indian context, where the main distinction is between soul (purusha, ātman) and the rest, including what Westerners classify as mental. This may need some explanation, and I shall return to the point in a moment. Meanwhile, the Sāṇkhya notion is that during the repose period the three guṇas are blended and in an inert state, save that like a small timebomb ticking away there are some karmic effects left over from the previous active kalpa which at the appropriate juncture begin a process of slight disequilibrium which soon begins to mount in intensity. Thus first some of the sattva is differentiated out, forming subtle entities such as intellects, and minds. With the domination of blended sattva, interactions occur between rajas and tamas. Gradually bodies, including animal bodies, form and match up with mental components. In due course the world as we know it is formed, where the three qualities are re-distributed in discrete beings throughout the natural world known as prakṛiti. It is a bit like milk curdling, a transformation of a blend into a more clotted form of the same stuff. This picture of evolutionary transformation was used by many later interpretations of theism to explain the process of creation, as God reactivates the cosmos from kalpa to kalpa (see the parallel treatment in *Encyclopedia*, pp. 231–233).

4.3.7 The Sāṇkhya cosmology is similar to that of Buddhism and perhaps derived from the same milieu (reference will be made again to Buddhist cosmology in Units 5–7). In any event, this type of picture took a vital grip on the Hindu imagination. It is a view very different from that of the Semitic milieu out of which Christianity grew, and whereas the latter traditions may in certain ways stress more the majesty of God (though the Gītā's picture is, as we shall see, somewhat shattering), the Indian tradition sets men over against an amazing and indeed overwhelming universe. There is a question as to how far such conceptions influence religious thinking and the quest for liberation.

Question

What are the differences between Hindu and the ancient Biblical picture of the cosmos as described at the beginning of the *Genesis?* Do such differences mean anything spiritually, and in relation to salvation?

PLEASE PAUSE HERE

DO NOT READ ON UNTIL YOU HAVE COMPLETED THE EXERCISE

Specimen answer

4.3.8 The ancient Biblical picture of the universe was of a world a few thousand years old, created suddenly by God, out of nothing. The cosmos was perceived as like an inverted colander resting on a flat disc, itself poised above a rather ill-defined chaos of waters. Through the colander came waters from above. Men were thought of as living hopefully three score years and ten, and might have a future existence—in later pre-Christian Judaism this was seen in terms of resurrection and the reshaping of the world. By contrast traditional Indian thinking has seen the heaven and earth of our world as one vast number of world systems; while the cosmos is of virtually infinite dualism, pulsating (as we have seen) through immense kalpas. Men, like other living beings, are continuously reborn in one form or another, including becoming denizens of foul purgatories or inhabitants of lovely though ultimately impermanent heavens. Only if they can gain a means of transcending the round of rebirth can men gain salvation. And that is either through strenuous austerity and yoga, or by God's grace.

4.3.9 The differing pictures matter somewhat in regard to the integration of myth and science. Though archaic in certain aspects, the Indian cosmology is much closer to the models and assumptions of modern science, the doctrine of rebirth apart. The enormous time-span and spatial scale of the universe in the ancient Indian imagination perhaps dwarfed man, and made the process of salvation seem highly strenuous—so it turns out to be even in the relatively moderate asceticism of the Buddhist path. The Indian emphasis on extreme mortification of the flesh perhaps stems from the picture of the cosmos. On the other hand, in the small world of the Bible man looms large, as co-worker with God: so salvation is increasingly seen in terms of a purpose running through men's short history. Interestingly, the linear sequence of the Christian Scriptures, from Adam through the second Adam (Christ) to the second coming, gives a sense of a plan to God's creation. The Indian cosmology is more inclined towards a picture of God everlastingly creating and recreating the universe in an exuberant self-expressive dance, as with the famous symbol of Śiva Natarāja, with many arms and legs, dancing out his meaning.

4.4 Chapter I of the Gītā

However, the Sāṇkhya is only one motif in the Gītā. Let us now move to comment more directly. In doing so I select out certain verses only but it is also important to read through the chapters reprinted in the *Reader*, §§2.6.1–2.6.5 'Bhagavad-Gītā Chapters I, II, VII, XI and XVIII'. Moreover, if, later, you have time I recommend you to read the translation of either Edgerton[1] or Radhakrishnan[2]; or alternatively there is the delightful verse rendering by Sir Edwin Arnold,[3] which is also reprinted with Edgerton's translation and commentary.

The opening sequence of the Gītā finds Arjuna poised to fight, but in an internecine battle in which he is likely to kill his own kinsman. It is his duty, and yet his mind is clouded by doubt and apprehension. He is comforted and advised by his charioteer, who is Kṛishṇa in disguise, who in turn is Vishṇu in disguise. Chapter I gives the flavour of the Epic Style, and shows Arjuna's depression.

4.5 Chapter II verses 17 and 19

4.5.1 In Chapter II, Kṛishṇa begins the task of teaching Arjuna a deeper truth than he can as yet see. Two verses are particularly significant, namely 17 and 19. Verse 17 is as follows:

> You must realise that that which pervades the whole universe cannot be destroyed. No one can cause destruction of the imperishable one.

4.5.2 So first Kṛishṇa seems to speak of the earthlessness of God who pervades the world. Is this being the same as the soul within each living being? This is the big question of interpretation of the Gītā as well as the Upanishads, as we shall see when we come to look at rival Vedānta expositions (in Unit 4).

4.5.3 Consider verse 17 in conjunction with verse 19, which is as follows:

> He who thinks this slays and he who thinks this is slain—both of them have no insight. There is no killer, no one is killed.

[1] Edgerton, F. (1944) *The Bhagavadgītā*, Harvard University Press.
[2] Radhakrishnan, S. (1948) *The Bhagavadgītā*, Allen & Unwin, London.
[3] Arnold, E. (1961) *The Song Celestial*, Routledge & Kegan Paul, London.

It may be, as Radhakrishnan says in his commentary, that the author is concerned simply with the relationship between the eternal and the non-eternal, the self and the not-self, in accordance with the Sāṇkhya distinction between purusha and prakṛiti (see §4.3 above). But a corollary of that view would be that there are many selves, not just one inherent in all, as verse 17 might seem to indicate. Kṛishṇa is saying, to put the matter in Western terms, one of two things, according to the two interpretations. He might (first) be saying:

> Anyone killing another person who thinks the other is killed is ignorant, for God is the essence of both parties, and God cannot be killed.

Or he might (second) be saying:

> Anyone who kills another person and thinks the other is killed is ignorant for in that person is an eternal soul which cannot be killed.

4.5.4 But whatever view we take note something vital, often overlooked, *there is no killer*. It sounds of course cold and a licence for unimaginable cruelty, for if there is no killer no crime is committed. The soul somehow lies beyond all responsibility. Since Kṛishṇa is more or less telling Arjuna that he might as well ride into battle, even against his kith and kin, for he will not truly be a killer, the teaching of Kṛishṇa seems at first sight to be immoral; and also an odd thing for Mahatma Gandhi to take with seriousness and love seeing that he was a foremost exponent of non-violence. Still, Krishna appears to be preparing the way for some further ideas. At this stage he has established, rather dramatically, the utter independence of the soul, rightly considered, from the material and social constraints which seem to most of us to hedge it round. This first lesson prepares for others, in the course of Kṛishṇa's line of teaching in the Gītā—which is perhaps not altogether consistent and certainly complex.

4.5.5 The point about souls can be put diagrammatically. Is Kṛishṇa saying that all men and God ('or the Absolute') share the same soul or is it that men's souls are like the soul which is God? On one hypothesis, the situation is as shown in Figure 5 where all souls are part of the one soul. An alternative hypothesis is shown in Figure 6 (see below). Here God is creator of the world and souls of living beings depend on him. In one picture they are identical, though limited. In the other picture they are different and dependent. That is a major question for the interpretation of these verses.

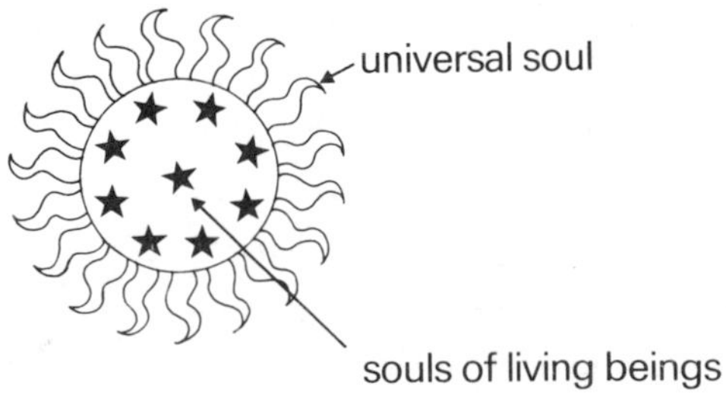

Figure 5

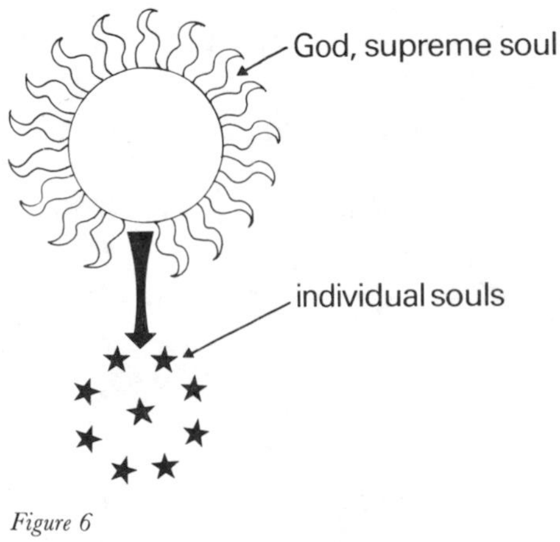

Figure 6

4.6 Chapter II verse 45

The first lesson, then, that Arjuna learns is the indestructibility of the soul. Second, he has to learn to act without regard to karmic consequences, unlike some who follow Vedic rituals in order to attain enjoyment and power. Indeed the Gītā in places seems very anti-ritualist and critical of Brāhmaṇical orthodoxy. Thus in verse 45 the text is:

> The Vedas concern the sphere of the three guṇas: but Arjuna you should free yourself from the three guṇas: be free from duality [*alternatively,* 'be indifferent to pleasure and pain'], established in eternal goodness, not caring for goods of this world, self-possessed.

This verse explains that the sphere of operation of the Vedic ritual is nature, i.e. the sphere of material blessings (even heaven counts as such, for the heavenly world is here looked on as a part of prakṛiti). But Arjuna will not achieve true liberation till he rises above such concerns. Note that one expression used means 'established (*stho*) in goodness (sattva)'. This may be a reference to the sattva guṇa, on the grounds that by generating as much brightness in one's intellect one can, according to Yoga, reflect the true self and so acquire release. In other words one paradoxically makes use of the guṇas in transcending them. The next verse (46) continues the critique of Vedic literalism: the Vedas are as much used as a pond in a flood for the Brāhmaṇ who truly understands the nature of the self.

4.7 Chapter II verses 58 and 61

The latter part of the chapter concerns the life of the true sage, and thus a picture of the yogi is drawn as in verse 58:

> He who withdraws his senses from objects of sense in all directions, as a tortoise withdraws its limbs, has his insight well established.

In the original text the last line uses the term *prajñā* (sometimes also translated 'wisdom')—a term which is central to Buddhist teaching; and there is a further overtone to Buddhist thought in verse 72, where the highest state is referred to as *brahma-nirvānam*, or holy *nirvāna*. (The Buddhist understanding of nirvāna will be discussed in Units 5–7.) However, though many of the verses in this later section could come straight out of the Buddhist *Dhammapada*, Kṛishṇa does in fact slip in something uncharacteristic of either Buddhism or classical Yoga in verse 61.

> Having brought all his senses under control, he should stay firm in yoga, intent upon me: for the person whose senses are under his command has an established insight.

The crucial expression here occurs in the second line—*matparah*, meaning 'intent on me'. As we shall see, this is in line with the culminating teachings of the Gītā. For ultimately yoga and action should be related to God.

4.8 Chapter III

However, for Arjuna there remains a puzzlement. On the one hand Kṛishṇa is urging him into battle; while on the other hand he is recommending yogic practices of withdrawal. How can one be both a warrior and a yogi? Kṛishṇa's reply is twofold. First yoga itself is a form of action. But second, and more importantly, it is the performance of duty in an altruistic spirit and for the sake of God.

Thus in Chapter III verse 30 Kṛishṇa says:

> Resigning all your karmas to me, with your consciousness fixed in the self, free from desire and selfishness, fight, freed from your fever.

So in this Kṛishṇa urges the path of action, the *karma-yoga*, and comes at it from two directions. Since the eternal self is unaffected by action, the wise man acts solely for duty's sake; and is unencumbered by egoism. But also by renouncing the fruits of action he does everything for the sake of God (who later on in the Gītā will be seen as the source of liberation).

4.9 Chapters IV to IX

4.9.1 However, the ideal of wisdom or spiritual knowledge remains important and so Kṛishṇa goes on, in Chapter IV (not included in your Reader selections), to outline the second path, namely *jñāna-yoga*. The term *jñāna* is an important one. Etymologically it relates to the Greek *gnosis* and the English 'know'. But it is not, at least in the context of religion and yoga, used for what is sometimes called discursive knowledge, like a knowledge of geography or algebra. Rather it has to do with direct insight into the nature of ultimate reality. Those movements flourishing both outside and inside early Christianity known as Gnosticism are so called because likewise they emphasize this gnosis.[1]

This higher insight, says Kṛishṇa, completely destroys all karmic effects and brings about liberation—and in a somewhat extravagant image he states (verse 36):

> Even if you should be the most evil of evil people you will cross over all evil by the boat of wisdom alone.

4.9.2 In the central part of the Gītā, in Chapters VII, VIII and IX in particular, Kṛishṇa expounds the theology which lies behind his practical advice. Thus in Chapter VII, he remarks that there is an eight-fold division of nature—earth, water, fire, air, ether (space), manas, intellect (*buddhi*) and the sense of identity. This last is the sense which gives unity to the individual person. This analysis of prakṛiti refers to Kṛishṇa's lower nature. It should be noted that often Indian religious thought sees the manifest universe as part of God. This does not imply a form of pantheism, as some Western critics of Hinduism are inclined to make out; but results from a particular view about God's creative causation. As can be seen from the creation stories in the Upanishads (see *Reader*, §§2.5.13–2.5.16), the creation is often depicted as a self-transformation by God. This is in accordance with Sāṇkhya and later theistic theory of causation, namely *satkāryavāda* (i.e., the theory that the effect is identical with the cause). Here the model of causation is a change occurring in a substance, for example, milk turning into curds, or the sky changing colour. So God is

[1] Gnosticism conceived of salvation by means of initiation into divine wisdom and the means of self knowledge.

bringing the cosmos into being transforms himself—hence the notion that the universe is God's body or lower nature (a doctrine which is central to Rāmānuja's doctrine, as we shall see in Unit 4, §3.3). Actually, because Kṛishṇa explicitly espouses the theory of kalpas and its attendant notion of periods of quiescence between each period of recreation and collapse, nature exists in two forms, latent and manifest. But Kṛishṇa is quite explicit about his higher, transcendent nature. Thus (Chapter VII verse 13) he states:

> Deluded by the three guṇas all this living world does not recognize me, who am above them and imperishable.

4.9.3 Thus Kṛishṇa or God in imperishable form is the source of the creation (and the dissolution) of the visible universe. But the wise can see God, being disciplined to the eternal, and single minded in bhakti.

4.9.4 However, there are those who worship other gods; but the fruit of such worship is temporary, for only the true God is changeless and imperishable. Note here a typical Indian theme—other gods are not derided as they would be in the Semitic religious traditions, but devalued. For both in Buddhism and the Gītā gods are figured as part of the universe and so themselves perishable. Hence in Chapter III verse 16 we have the following verse:

> From the world of Brahmā downwards, all worlds are subject to return to rebirth; but on reaching me, son of Kunbī [Arjuna] there is no return to birth again.

4.9.5 So even the realm of the great god Brahmā, creator god of the Brāhmaṇ class, is impermanent. But Kṛishṇa in his nature somehow incorporates the imperishable in his being, and this is rather beautifully described in Chapter VIII verse 9:

> The person will be saved who meditates upon the seer, the ancient one, the governor, subtler than the subtle, supporter of the whole, whose form is beyond conception, who is sun-coloured beyond the darkness.

4.9.6 The divine Person is seer, because omniscient, and he is both the great lord of all and tinier than the atom. Here there are echoes of the ideas of the Īśā. But also he is sun-coloured beyond the darkness. Radhakrishnan comments about this that God is light as opposed to darkness; but I think something deeper is indicated, namely that the nature of God is seen in mystical experience, gnosis (Unit 4, §§2.3–2.5). One may refer to the rather mysterious lines of the Īśā Upaṇishad verse 9:

> Into blind darkness enter those who worship ignorance; but into even greater darkness go those who delight in knowledge.

4.9.7 It will be seen that the word for knowledge here is *vidyā*, a key term for Śaṅkara and Advaita Vedānta (as we shall see in Unit 4, §§2.3–2.5), and a term which like jñāna signifies spiritual knowledge and thus gnosis. The meaning of the verse may be that in the yogic journey into the depths of the soul a person enters a state in which all distinctions are lost. And yet also what is found is luminous; hence the reference to God in the Gītā passage as 'sun-coloured'. The Christian mystic Ruysbroeck[1] refers to the mystical state as 'dazzling obscurity' and this may be the meaning too of the Gītā. (However, the verse may only mean that those who delight in worldly knowledge, cleverness, go into great darkness or ignorance).

4.10 Chapter XI verse 3

4.10.1 However, God is not merely the transcendent goal of the mystic, but shows himself in amazing numinous power. This is brought out by the fearful poetry in Chapter XI. This is one of the most powerful—perhaps *the* most powerful—description of a theophany in the whole religious literature of the world, and is a prime example of what Rudolf Otto called the numinous. In his book *The Idea of the Holy*[2] he sketched what he saw as the central kind of religious experience, of God as a holy, awe-inspiring being, a *mysterium tremendum atque fascinans,* a tremendous and fascinating mystery (remembering that the primary sense of 'tremendous' is 'making one tremble', as with an uncanny fear). If the natural response to Vishṇu as imperishable and changeless being is the yogic quest for interior knowledge of the divine truth, the natural response to the numinous theophany of God is worship, and beyond that (because for all his fearsomeness this is loving) devotion.

4.10.2 At the start of Chapter XI, Arjuna having heard from Kṛishṇa his theology and theory of himself, now wants to see God as he really is. Thus he addresses God as follows:

> You have said how you are in yourself, supreme Lord.
> But I desire to see your bodily form, O supreme Person.

Here Arjuna addressed Kṛishṇa as *parameśvara* (i.e. *parama*, supreme, *īśvara* Lord) and God is seen explicitly as a personal being, not as a somewhat impersonal light in the interior vision of the yogi. But God needs to give Arjuna the divine eye, a special supernatural means of perception, before the theophany can occur. This conception of a divine eye is found also in Buddhism; but its application here in the Gītā is an important reflection of a view about revelation which occurs in a number of religious traditions—namely that only God can give knowledge of himself: men cannot know him save in so far as he reveals himself. Knowledge of, or the vision of, the Lord is given by the Lord. This fits in with the Gītā's doctrine of grace, in which salvation also is seen as the gift of God, not an achievement by the individual. So the theophany paves the way for the central doctrine of liberation, culminating in the last chapter.

Question

Why is it, if God is loving, he can appear so fierce? Base your answer on your reading of Bhagavad-Gītā, Chapter XI verse 24 to the end of the chapter.

PLEASE PAUSE HERE
DO NOT READ ON UNTIL YOU HAVE COMPLETED THE EXERCISE

[1] Van Ruysbroeck, J. (1293–1381) was a Flemish mystic.
[2] Otto, R. (1968) *The Idea of the Holy* (trans Harvey, J. W.) Oxford University Press.

Specimen answer

4.10.3 God is seen as majestic, and if that is so then men are dwarfed by his power. It is therefore natural for him to seem overwhelming. Further, if Otto is right,[1] a vitally important religious experience is of awe, and thus the somewhat fierce descriptions of God are a symbolic means of expressing the 'tremendum' aspect of the Holy. In addition, Vishṇu is seen as Time, the destroyer, for everything in the cosmos is impermanent, and so it is logical to think of God not just as creator but also as destroyer. In the immediate context of the battle about to be joined the warriors destined to die will be mown down in effect by God, for the whole world is in his power, including the human agents whose minds and bodies are after all, just part of prakṛiti, nature. The problem of evil is not solved but simply presented as part of the way the world is; and in a way this is better than hiving off evil to a Devil who after all is a creature of God and so his ultimate responsibility. But if God is destructive he is also compassionate, and liberation comes from his favour to those who take refuge in him. It is logical therefore that it is by God's act that people are not saved, or rather their salvation posponed, for the Gītā does not argue for eternal perdition, but instead for maybe hellish, but impermanent, future existences; or to use a Western term, purgatories. So from these various angles God can be seen as both frightening and loving, both 'tremendum' and 'fascinans'.

4.11 Chapter XVIII verses 61 and 62

4.11.1 As we have seen, the response to God's majesty is worship and adoration. These culminate in the attitude of bhakti and the path of *bhakti-yoga*. The final and main teaching of the Gītā concerns the reciprocal relationship between bhakti and God's grace.

The final chapter of the Gītā recapitulates some of the essential Sāṇkhya emphases, but goes on to a strong portrayal of Kṛishṇa's power to save. Thus in Chapter XVIII verses 61 and 62, we have the following:

> The Lord exists in the hearts of all beings, Arjuna, and makes them turn round by his magic power as if they were mounted on a machine.
>
> Go to him therefore with all your being, Bhārata; thus by his grace you shall attain the highest peace and an eternal abode.

4.11.2 In the second of these verses there are some key terms. First, Kṛishṇa is described as *śaraṇa*, a refuge, a term used of the Buddha. The idea of highest peace, etc., is also reminiscent of Buddhist language. However the most vital term is *prasāda* which can be translated 'grace' though it also is used of a portion of food which sanctified by being given to a god is distributed as a kind of sacred offering to the faithful. At any rate the message is a clear one—that God reciprocates faith with grace which brings salvation. And in what does this salvation consist? The Gītā is not altogether explicit, except negatively. Negatively, salvation is *from* the round of saṁsāra and the troubles which beset living beings in this world. Positively, matters are vaguer, but the suggestion is that somehow liberated souls home in, as it were, on Vishṇu. Whether that means that souls realize identity with the Divine or whether it means that they live separately from,

prasada — grace.

[1] Otto, R. (1968) *ibid.*, Chapter 1.

but in close union with, God in eternal bliss, is a matter of interpretation. But for many Hindus the supreme blessing is a life in Vishṇu's heaven.

4.11.3 Though some Upanishads, notably the *Katha*, are more explicitly theistic than others, there is no doubt of a shift of feeling as between the Vedic writings and the Gītā. The greater numinosity of the Lord in the latter is evident; but more importantly the piety of the Kṛishṇa and *Vaishṇavite* tradition was clear (on this tradition see *Encyclopedia*, p. 224) and brought with it a powerful emphasis on bhakti, which was to remain vital through the rest of classical and medieval Hinduism. It needs noting too that such bhakti was also directed at Śiva, especially in the southern medieval period. To that we shall return, when we come to discuss the background to Rāmānuja's theology.

4.12 The final verses

Possibly the last verses of the Gītā are a later addition. But they are still significant in relation to Indian spirituality. To the book itself, as to the *Lotus Sūtra* in Mahāyāna Buddhism, salvific powers are ascribed.

In Chapter XVIII verse 71 Kṛishṇa states that the person who listens to it with faith and without scoffing will attain to the happy worlds of the righteous. And Arjuna declares (in verse 75) that by the grace of the sage Vyasa, legendary composer of the Epic and so of the Gītā he has heard a supreme mystery. Here and elsewhere the imagery of hearing, śruti, and so revelation is emphasized; and a note at the end of the word indicates that the Gītā itself is an Upanishad. So though not formally recognized as revelation, the poem claims and has gained powerful authority within the religious life of India. Thus the stage was set for the further development of a strong theism which has been one of the main motifs of Hinduism, from the classical period through till modern times, even if it also lived side by side with atheistic systems such as Sāṇkhya and Jainism, and with a system, Advaita Vedānta, which accepted theism only up to a point.

śruti - what is heard.

(a)

(b)

Figure 7 (a)–(f) Scenes from the Rāmāyana. *Rāma is a human hero and the seventh incarnation of Vishṇu. (a) shows Rāma with his wife Sita and his devoted half-brother Lakhsman, discoursing with the sage Valmiki who is said to have composed the epic of Rāma, the* Rāmāyana, *in the fifth century* BC. *(b) shows Rāma successfully completing the task set by Sita's father for suitors to win the hand of the beautiful princess. Rāma is first shown lifting, then bending and finally breaking the great bow of Śiva. (c) shows the triumphal procession of the bridal couple. But sadness lies in wait for them.*

(c)

(d)

(e)

(f)

(d) Through courtly intrigue Rāma loses is rightful inheritance of the throne in favour of Bharata. Bharata himself upholds the right of Rāma and pleads in vain with him not to go into exile. In exile further sadness awaits Rāma. His beloved wife is abducted by the wicked, ten-headed Ravana. Ravana's defeat is the very purpose of this avatāric form. (e) shows the god, Rāma aided both by Lakhsman and Hanuman, the monkey god, slaying Ravana. In (f) the god and his companions are shown at ease in a garden after the battle. But even here the story is not over, for Rāma is consumed by jealousy lest Sita should have been unfaithful in her captivity. But Sita, the Indian ideal of the loving faithful wife finally convinces her doubting husband of her never-failing faithfulness. (Photos a, d, f by kind permission of Baroda Museum; b, c, by kind permission Prince of Wales Museum, Delhi; photos by Bury Peerless.)

5 The formation of classical Hinduism 800 BC–100 CE

5.1 Traditional and unorthodox developments

5.1.1 We may now sum up certain tendencies in the crucial period from 800 BC to about 100 CE when classical Hinduism was in process of formation. First, the infusion of yogic techniques into Brāhmaṇical ritualism, and the growth of belief in a unitary divine Being found a synthesis in the Upanishads. Meanwhile doctrines of rebirth, karma and kalpas were absorbed into the Sanskrit tradition, giving a new view of the problem of moksha or liberation. While various unorthodox movements rejected the Vedic tradition, other revolutions within what was forming itself into Hinduism proper were occurring, one being the welling up of a strongly devotional attachment to certain gods, notably the avatars or incarnation of Vishṇu–Rāma and Kṛishṇa. Also in this period there was a stronger emergence of the cult of the powerful Śiva, so that with Vishṇu he was due to be a main representation of the supreme God of Hinduism. At the same period traditional Hindu law came to be formulated decisively in the *Manusmṛiti* (or Laws or Manu); and the various main motifs of ancient Hinduism came to be interrelated—the practice of one's duty, including religious duties, within the framework of varṇa and jāti (this was in a way Arjuna's problem—how honourably to fulfil his duties as a warrior); the practice of yoga leading to jñāna or gnosis; and the devotional worship of one's God, or bhakti. A main reason for the enduring influence of the Bhagavad-Gītā is that it provided a synthesis between the three paths of karma, jñāna and bhakti.

5.1.2 In all this one can perceive a process which has been at work through much of the history of Hinduism—the attempt to incorporate new elements into a general fabric of belief and life. Though as we saw the Gītā is critical of Vedic ritualism, it is nevertheless a work which has been used and interpreted by Brahmins. Of course, it is more widely available to the masses, even those beyond the upper three classes (see §1.6 (a) above) who alone are supposed to have access to śruti, (i.e. 'what is heard', see §1.3 above).

5.1.3 But it is also a way of incorporating into the Upanishadic tradition the revolutionary bhakti religion addressed to Kṛishṇa and Vishṇu, as well as aspects of Sāṇkhya and Yoga which initially lay (probably) outside the orthodox āstika tradition. It also prepared the way for medieval Indian theism, so formative of Hindu piety, and (despite the successes of Advaita) still the most vital aspect of modern Hinduism.

5.2 A concluding question

5.2.1 By way of conclusion on this unit, it might be good to list ten verses from the Gītā which seem to give the gist of its message; they can be selected from Chapters I, II, VII, XI and XVIII. Which verses would you choose? What important themes would you include?

PLEASE PAUSE HERE

DO NOT READ ON UNTIL YOU HAVE COMPLETED THIS EXERCISE

Specimen answer and discussion

5.2.2 I would choose Chapter I verse 46, Chapter II verse 19, Chapter II verse 38, Chapter VII verse 7, Chapter VII verse 28, Chapter XI verse 38, Chapter XI verse 55, Chapter XVIII verse 11, Chapter XVIII verse 65 and Chapter XVIII verse 77. But that is only one selection.

Two themes left out in the above selection concern varṇa (class, framework for the later more elaborated caste system)—for the Gītā in fact defends the Hindu *status quo*. First, that Arjuna should perform his duty, as a warrior, despite his hesitations about killing relatives, as part of a wider injunction to perform one's duties according to one's fixed station in life. Second, the quotations do not stress the Sāṇkhya theory built in to the Gītā's thinking, especially the idea of the three guṇas or qualities which are the basis not only for a psychology but also the theory of the development of the cosmos under the guidance of God.

Also, the verses are not very favourable to a non-dualist (Advaitin) interpretation of the Gītā, as formed by Śaṅkara (see Unit 4, §2.1–2.5).

Figure 8 Rāma with his bow. Sixteenth century Vijayangar/Nayyak, Madras. (Crown copyright. Victoria and Albert Museum.)

6 Further reading

Basham, A. L. (1954) *The Wonder that was India*, Sidgwick & Jackson, London.

Daniélou, A. (1964) *Hindu Polytheism,* Routledge & Kegan Paul, London.

Edgerton, F. (1944) *The Bhagavadgītā* (2 vols), Harvard University Press.

Hinnells, J. and Sharpe, E. (1972) *Hinduism,* Oriel Press, London.

Radhakrishnan, S. (1963) *The Principal Upanishads*, Allen & Unwin, London.

Radhakrishnan, S. (1948) *The Bhagavadgītā*, Allen & Unwin, London.

Zaehner, R. C. (1962) *Hinduism,* Oxford University Press.

Zimmer, H. (1957) *The Philosophies of India*, Dewer Books, London.

Unit 4

CLASSICAL HINDU PHILOSOPHY AND THEOLOGY

Written by Ninian Smart for the Course Team

Contents

1 Historical development

1.1 The self and Brahman

By way of introduction to your study of Classical Hindu Philosophy and Theology you should read the concise treatment in your set books, especially *Encyclopedia*,[1] pages 230–235.

1.1.1 If the period from about the third century BC through to the third century CE saw the emergence of Hindu religion in its classical form, incorporating theistic devotion, a syncretism of gods, the cult of images and the building of temples, it also saw the systematization of Hindu thought. Partly this was achieved through the writing of *sūtras*. These are aphoristic texts which set forth a given system. (For the meaning of the term see *Encyclopedia*, pp. 232–233) Thus the *Yoga-sūtra* of *Patañjali* sets forth the principles of the Yoga school. Other schools had similar texts. Because of the urge to make each aphorism as brief as possible, the sūtras are in many places unintelligible without a commentary; and further they are often ambiguous for the same reason. Hence there can be wide divergences of interpretation. This is nowhere more evident than in relation to the classical summation of *Vedānta*, which is found in the text known as the *Brahma Sūtra*, 'Aphorisms concerning the Holy Power'. (You will find an informative account of the Brahma Sūtra, which contains the essence of Upanishadic teaching, in *Encyclopedia*, p. 233) The date when it was put together is in dispute, but possibly it was composed as late as the sixth century CE, by *Bādarāyana*. But it became the subject of some great commentaries, notably those of *Śaṅkara* and *Rāmānuja;* and was the central formulation of the Vedānta tradition—for which reason it is also known as the *Vedānta Sūtra*. The classical period also saw the emergence of some powerful forms of Buddhist thinking. Notable among these was the *Mādhyamika* philosophy of *Nāgārjuna* (who flourished around 100 CE), which was influential upon Śaṅkara, as we shall see (§2.1 below). You will meet these aspects of Buddhist thought again in Units 5–7. In the meanwhile you may wish to refer to the philosophy of Mādhyamika in *Encyclopedia*, pp. 311–313 for some points of comparison between this and Hindu philosophy.

1.1.2 As was noted in the discussion of the *Bhagavad-Gītā*, the most vital theological question concerning its interpretation, and indeed the interpretation of the Upanishads, had to do with the relationship between the self and God (Unit 3, §4.9). Were they identical or not? The famous phrase of the *Chāndogya Upanishad* VII; 13 (*Encyclopedia*, p. 230), for instance, seemed to imply identity, where Svetaketu's father says to him *tat satyam sā ātmā tat tvam asi*: 'That is the true; this is the self; that art thou.' This is one of the so-called great sayings (*mahāvākya*) of the Upanishads, and interpreted straightforwardly is the main peg upon which Śaṅkara hung his non-dualism.

1.1.3 As well as the question of the self and Brahman, there is also the question of how each relates to the world, i.e. the natural world other than the selves or self implicated in it. Again, there is a question of whether any

[1] Zaehner, R. C. (ed) (1988) *The Hutchinson Encyclopedia of Living Faiths*, Rev edition, Century Hutchinson, London (set book), hereafter cited as *Encyclopedia*.

identity between God and the world can be postulated. As we shall see, these questions are not just theoretical, but relate very closely to the type of religion promoted by the different thinkers. Of these thinkers and systems the most important are Śaṅkara, Rāmānuja and Madhva (ninth, twelfth and thirteenth centuries CE respectively), all South Indians, who argued respectively for non-dualism or *Advaita*, qualified non-dualism or *Viśishṭādvaita* and dualism, *Dvaita*—the titles having to do with the relationship between Brahman and the self. (See Unit 3, §3.5. For further information on these thinkers, see *Encyclopedia*, pp 234–236; their thought is considered more fully in §§2.3 and 4.1–4.3 below.)

1.1.4 Question

Consider what combinations of relationships are possible between God, soul and world, if one is identical (or not) with both or either of the others.

PLEASE PAUSE HERE
DO NOT READ ON UNTIL YOU HAVE COMPLETED THE EXERCISE

Specimen answer

The combinations seem to be as follows (I use $\equiv$ and $\not\equiv$ respectively to symbolize identity and difference):

1 God $\equiv$ soul; soul $\not\equiv$ world (thus God $\not\equiv$ world)
2 God $\equiv$ soul; soul $\equiv$ world (thus God $\equiv$ world)
3 God $\not\equiv$ soul; soul $\not\equiv$ world; God $\not\equiv$ world)
4 God $\not\equiv$ soul; soul $\equiv$ world (thus God $\not\equiv$ world)
5 God $\not\equiv$ soul; soul $\not\equiv$ world; God $\equiv$ world)

There are other possible combinations e.g.

6 God $\equiv$ soul (in part)
7 God $\equiv$ world (in part)

Since the philosophical positions are qualified in subtle ways, only roughly do these formulae correspond to the positions of the thinkers we have mentioned; but 3 is closest to Madhva; and according to variations of interpretation 1 and 2 correspond to Advaita; Brahman has only a lower aspect which is personal and so should not, perhaps, be translated as God; 5 is one way of representing Rāmānuja.

Page 234 Encyclopaedia

1.1.5 The difficulty facing those who wished to interpret the Upanishadic tests—and the same could be said in regard to the Bhagavad-Gītā—was the apparent conflict between such statements as that quoted above, 'That art thou', and other statements implying some sort of difference between God and the soul. Thus there was an underlying urge to produce some version of what was called *bhedābhedavāda*, or the doctrine of identity-in-difference, so that Brahman could be seen both as identical with and different from the *ātman* (and from *prakṛiti*, the natural world, see Unit 3, §3.5). Naturally such a compromise was likely to be unstable, and was in essence rejected, from different directions, by Śaṅkara and Madhva. Rāmānuja's theology was an ingenious attempt to make it viable. Since it is plausible to hold that Bāḍarāyana himself held a version of bhedābhedavāda, there is reason to consider Rāmānuja's system closest to the spirit of the Brahma Sūtra. But it undoubtedly is Śaṅkara's Advaita that has had the greatest influence in modern times. Let us pause here to consider the rediscovery of Indian philosophy in the nineteenth and twentieth centuries, for it is important in estimating approaches such as that of S. Radhakrishnan, who has been such an important mediator of the Indian intellectual tradition to the English-speaking world.

1.2 The influence of Advaita

1.2.1 For various reasons Indian philosophy lost much of its creative vigour from about the fourteenth century onwards. Partly this was because of the impact of Islamic culture and partly because of the later rather chaotic situation during the disintegration of the Mughal empire and the conquest of the sub-continent by the British. One of the effects of this last situation was the substitution of a form and style of education different from the old Brāhmanical Sanskrit tradition, through the creation, in the nineteenth century of English-speaking universities. Meanwhile, Western

Figure 1 Temple spires on the Ganges where pilgrims bathe every morning at Varanasī (Banares). (Douglas Dickins.)

orientalists were beginning to collect, edit and translate the classical Indian works. All this led to a wider availability of the sources of Indian philosophy. One or two Western philosophers made direct use of Indian themes, notably Artur Schopenhauer. Further, it happened that in Europe and later in Britain the most dominant philosophy was Idealism, most influentially and magisterially expressed by Hegel.

1.2.2 This outlook involved seeing the world as permeated by and a product of an Absolute Mind. (Marx, by making matter the basic stuff of reality, turned Hegel on his head.) The analogy between Hegel and Advaita Vedānta was rapidly perceived, and formed the basis of a synthesis between Eastern and Western thought congenial to the new generation of Indian intellectuals. It was also a means of interpreting Hinduism as an enlightened, both ancient and modern, religion—a task rendered important to Indian pride by the critical assault on Hindu customs and beliefs by missionaries and reforming administrators. Here then is a factor in the great influence which forms of Advaita have had in the interpretation of Indian philosophical and religious history. Some of the most vital figures in modern India have made use of Advaitin themes—Vivekananda, Aurobindo and Radhakrishnan himself.

2 Śaṅkara and the two levels of truth

2.1 Sūnyavāda and māyā

2.1.1 Śaṅkara is supposed to have lived from 788 to 820 CE. If indeed he died so young he packed a tremendous amount into such a short life. (*Encyclopedia,* pp. 233–234 should be read in conjunction with the following account of Śaṅkara, especially Basham's treatment of his teaching as the standard philosophy of intellectual Hinduism.) Of his philosophical works, the most important are his great commentaries on the Brahma Sūtra and on the Gītā. But in addition he also wrote spiritual treatises and hymns. His literary and dialectical activities were supplemented by an energetic programme of religious revival, including the setting up of monastic foundations in different parts of India (Śaṅkara's successors as heads of the order still take the title *Śāṅkarācārya,* viz. 'Teacher Śaṅkara' for the title *acārya* was accorded to Śaṅkara himself). At any rate, his system had immediate impact and was a major factor in the revival of Hinduism over and against its chief rival, Buddhism. Partly this was because Śaṅkara made some use of Buddhist themes; and for this reason was called by his Hindu critics a crypto-Buddhist.

I referred to his debt to the Mahayana Buddhist philosopher Nāgārjuna. (For further reference to Nāgārjuna, *see Encyclopedia*, pp. 294–295. Let me recapitulate briefly Nāgārjuna's ideas. According to him the Buddha's teaching that everything is impermanent leads, when taken to its logical conclusion, to a religious and philosophical insight of profound significance. It means, when looked at in one way, that nothing has substance: what we know as reality is empty or *śūnya*, void. The mystic experiences this emptiness directly, and so is liberated from entanglement in the illusory world. That is the religious insight.

2.1.2 Philosophically, the matter can be expressed by saying that all views of reality are self-contradictory, for they all rely upon the idea of substance and more particularly of causation. Any way in which I try to understand how things happen in the world depends upon the notion that one thing causes another, but such a notion is self-contradictory, because if everything is radically impermanent, A will have ceased to exist before B begins to come into being; and something cannot be caused by what already is non-existent. By such arguments Nāgārjuna sought to establish the emptiness of all views. About reality nothing could be said. So philosophical argument was used in the service of ineffable mystical insight. However, Nāgārjuna was still faced with the question of the relation between his doctrine of the void, his *śūnyavāda*, and common sense experience. He did this with a device which Śaṅkara was due to exploit powerfully a few centuries later. It was the device of postulating two levels of truth, the higher (at which level truth is represented by the ineffable Void, which can be pointed to or hinted at but not discursively expressed), and the conventional level (where we make use of language for practical purposes). It follows that the discursive teaching even of the Buddha himself occurs at this lower level; and so is merely provisional.

Śaṅkara not only used his notion of two levels of truth but also gave a special Hindu interpretation of Nāgārjuna's idea of the insubstantiality of the world. Here he made use of the term *māyā*, commonly translated as 'illusion'. For Śaṅkara the world is māyā. The root of this view lies in his rigorous interpretation of *tat tvam asi*.

Question

What consequences follow if Brahman and the self are literally identical? (You will find a basis for an answer in *Encyclopedia*, p. 233 ff.)

PLEASE PAUSE HERE

DO NOT READ ON UNTIL YOU HAVE COMPLETED THE EXERCISE

Specimen answer

If Brahman is one, and if it be numerically identical with the ātman, then there can only be one ātman. It follows that the Self lying behind my mental states is identical with the Self lying behind yours. In this case, the sense of my being a separate self is an illusion. Another consequence of saying that Brahman and ātman are one is that insofar as Brahman is divine, I am in my essence divine. But this in turn means that the distinction which I make between myself and God when I worship him in the spirit of *bhakti* and in the atmosphere of the numinous is also an illusory one. In fact, my picture of God is deceptive; and so God conceived as *Īśvara*, Lord and creator of the universe is part of the grand illusion. This implies in turn that the whole world is of the nature of māyā. In truth, therefore, there is only one being, without a second and that is Brahman/ātman. This is the higher knowledge which Śaṅkara's philosophical theology is designed to establish.

2.1.3 The original sense of māyā as it occurs in the *Ṛig Veda* and some of the Upanishads refers to the creative power of a god or God. Sometimes it enables a god to transform himself; thus Indra is said to assume many shapes by the power of his māyā. From this, it was a natural evolution to think of māyā as magical, and from this again to see it as the power to create illusions, and then such an illusion itself. Thus by these transitions māyā came to have that sense which Śaṅkara had in mind. At the same time it allowed him to build a bridge between the ancient texts and his revolutionary doctrine. Thus God as wielder of māya, i.e. God as *māyin*, is both himself in the last resort an illusion and the creator of an illusory world.

2.1.4 There are three ways so far in which Śaṅkara does not treat the religious ultimate as Void, but rather as Being. Brahman may not be discursively defined, but he is the Real. (Here Śaṅkara stands firmly in the tradition of the great *mantra* or verse: 'Lead me from the unreal to the real).[1] Second, Śaṅkara gives a more magical, bewitching account of the created order: it is not just that it lacks substance; it is a vivid illusion. Third, because Śaṅkara approaches Mādhyamika from his own standpoint he may partly misrepresent it—for Nāgārjuna's critiques concern what we know rather than what is there (or is not).

2.2 Śaṅkara's doctrine of falsification

2.2.1 Strictly, the theory of two levels was understood by Śaṅkara to be three levels, in that within the conventional world of illusion (i.e. the lower

[1] *Bṛihad-āranyaka Upanishad* I.3.28.

level proper) there are two levels of illusion. Thus the mirage which the traveller sees in the desert is unreal even by unreal standards. It is an illusion within the grand illusion. The higher truth stands then to the world as the world to the mirage. The point is illustrated by the following story, no doubt apocryphal.

apocryphal - untrue - invented

> Śaṅkara at a certain period was giving instruction in philosophy and spiritual truth to a mahārāja. The prince however refused to believe that Śaṅkara in his bones could really subscribe to his own doctrine of the illusoriness of the world, and so decided to play a trick on him. He got his servants to release a wild elephant in the path of Ṣaṅkara one day as the latter was making his way to the palace for his usual session with the mahārāja. Śaṅkara rapidly scaled the nearest tree. The servants recaptured the beast, and gingerly Śaṅkara got down the tree and made his way to the palace. The king had observed his flight from the elephant from some bushes nearby, but was already back at the palace to welcome his distinguished young teacher upon his arrival. The mahārāja was smug. 'You did not, sir' he remarked, 'think that that elephant was an illusion'. Śaṅkara looked at the mahārāja with a mild but pitying look. 'I see, sire, that you are still in the grip of ignorance', he replied 'That was not me you saw flee from an elephant up a tree, but the appearance of me fleeing from an illusory elephant up an unreal tree'.

2.2.2 In brief, māyā is not literal illusion but is one by analogy, just as God is not literally a person but is so by analogy. Thus a person who attains liberation and realizes his identity with Brahman is like a person waking up after sleep—the reality of the dream vanishes. So, from the viewpoint of the higher consciousness, the world is illusion. But for nearly all of us, living within the world, it retains its reality. Śaṅkara justified this thesis with a doctrine of falsification—of what falsifies a belief or attitude. Thus if I think a rope is a snake I can continue to believe this till something in my experience contradicts the belief, such as the failure of the rope to move when trodden on. So until something in my experience contradicts my belief in the reality of the world I go on accepting it as genuine; but in the higher experience of knowing Brahman and relating my identity with it, I realize that what I took before as genuine is not so. In brief, my new experience contradicts and so falsifies what I used to take as natural and as the real thing. Thus Śaṅkara considered, to use modern terminology, that his interpetation of reality was empirical, for it rested upon intuitional experience, but not of course ordinary sense experience. Rather, it depended on that *gnosis* which we discussed in Unit 3, §4.9. Indeed it rested upon *jñāna* or *vidyā* (i.e. spiritual knowledge).

2.2.3 To sum up regarding māyā: the illusion postulated by Śaṅkara is, at the end of the day, illusion as seen from the higher reaches of mystical experience. Consequently even the God of bhakti, even the God revealed in the awesome theophany of the Gītā is transcended in the experience of higher unity.

theophany - a manifestation or appearance of deity to man.

2.3 The interpretation of contradictory texts

2.3.1 One vital aspect of the two-level theory of truth was that it enabled Śaṅkara in a bold strike to resolve the problems posed by the apparent inconsistencies of the Veda, including centrally the Upanishads, not to mention those contained in the Gītā. As has been indicated, while some of the Upanishads seem to stress the identity between Brahman and ātman (cf. Unit 3, §3.6), and to treat Brahman as relatively impersonal and non-dynamic, others are more personal and theistic in tone. Moreover, sometimes the life of interior contemplation and yoga is stressed, and yet logically the Upanishads are concerned with the meaning of the Brāhmaṇical sacrificial ritual. Sometimes in other respects they appear a bit of a jumble. Yet for the orthodox interpreter they were divinely revealed to the *ṛishi* or holy men of old, and were in fact everlasting truths which had been brought to the knowledge of seers and other men. Thus it was hardly open to Śaṅkara or any other commentator of the period to doubt this passage or that. The scriptures had to be taken as a unitary whole. Yet that, as we have seen, could cause problems because of the apparent inconsistencies. But the two-level theory of truth could swiftly resolve the problem, although at a cost.

2.3.2 Question

In what various ways can one deal with scripture interpretation (whether in the Hindu or other traditions), given that there are apparent inconsistencies internally or that new knowledge such as that yielded by the study of history or science may seem inconsistent with the scriptures? Try to set out briefly possible answers which may be given to these difficulties.

PLEASE PAUSE HERE

DO NOT READ ON UNTIL YOU HAVE COMPLETED THE EXERCISE

Specimen answer

(a) One can take the scriptures as simply revealed or everlastingly true, and strive to reconcile apparent contradictions at the same level of truth.

(b) One may hold that the scriptures are human creations but reflect divine revelation in part. Here the problem is how to light on a criterion for distinguishing the two aspects.

(c) One may reconcile the apparent contradictions between parts of scripture or between them and external knowledge by seeing them as involving different 'games' or styles of literature or language. For example, in the Christian tradition some portions of scripture have been treated literally, others as allegorical, etc.

(d) One may see portions of scripture as speaking at one level, others at another (as according to Śaṅkara).

(e) One may dismiss scriptures as not authoritative sources of divine or this-worldy truth (though they could be useful evidence for scholars getting at the historical facts, etc.)

In fact (b), (c) and (d) involve very similar tactics of intepretation. In a sense they combine in Śaṅkara's commentary, for he stresses experience (b), literary analysis (c) and his theory of truth (d).

2.3.3 So Śaṅkara's two-level theory enabled him to interpret texts in a consistent way. Thus if Text A appears to contradict Text B, then maybe A is at Level One and B at Level Two. Consider a parallel. Suppose a person is told to explore a railway tunnel but to keep his ears open for approaching trains. Halfway down the tunnel it is pitch black, but the person feels a quickening along the rails as though a train is coming. He might say to himself 'I can't see a thing, but I see what he meant'. The seeming contradiction is obviously and easily resolved. In the first sense of 'see' it is literal, in the second use it is at a different, metaphorical level of Truth. Similarly with Śaṅkara's approach to the texts. However, there was a cost, or at least what Śaṅkara's critics account to be a cost. If the higher truth referred to the reality of Brahman and of the experience of Brahman, most of what was involved in both the ordinary man's religion and the Brāhmaṇ's rituals (and most of the references to God and the Gods in the Vedic scriptures) belonged by the same token to the lower level of truth. To put it another way: bhakti, the greater part of the Veda, ritual religion—all these were part of the realm of illusion. So though Śaṅkara saw the Vedas as divinely authoritative, and though he saw them through the mahāvākyas or great sayings as pointing to ultimate truth, yet he could also be represented as minimizing the ritual of the Brāhmaṇs (though he was one himself).

2.3.4 Śaṅkara's two-level theory thus seemed to cost a lot. He sought an ingenious new method of interpreting the scriptures for the price of a fair amount of hostility from the orthodox. He could thus be seen as backing Buddhist scepticisms about Brāhmaṇ religion. However, this was far from correct, for Śaṅkara led to a revival of the very traditions he was accused of attacking.

Indeed he was still another example of the syncretic genius of Brāhmaṇical Hinduism, which has tended to absorb, not to reject, and so has acquired a greater dominance than rejection could bring about. And so Śaṅkara incorporated much of the Mahāyāna Buddhist philosophy into this thought. Nevertheless, it could be seen as a weakness of his doctrine that he fails fully to explain why one needs ritual and bhakti as a means to the higher realization which brings about liberation. Some modern thinkers are therefore, perhaps logical in considering Advaita as a perennial philosophy open to those of any religious tradition. So it could be that Śaṅkara's early critics were correct. (On the other hand, they doubtless could still be asked why adhere to one tradition, viz that of the Brāhmaṇs, rather than to any other.)

2.3.5 Also, in view of the fact that Śaṅkara took bhakti seriously enough to compose hymns to the personal *Īśvara* who was in the last resort part of the grand illusion, he must have taken the devotional approach to ultimate reality seriously. As an orthodox exponent of the Brahma Sūtra he valued the ritual tradition out of which the Upanishadic speculations were born. So he lived, like most Hindus, within the feeling that India itself was the world; and so he had (save for his encounter with Buddhist thought) no need to come to terms with the kind of plural world which we experience today, and which also is the background effectively of the course. So the question: 'Why accept śruti?' had to be answered only in a rather narrow context, and despite his debt to Buddhism he saw it as a deviant from the main tradition.

2.4 Liberation from ignorance

2.4.1 However, a main question about Śaṅkara's Advaita is still left unanswered. Why should he opt for the strict identity theory? One reason

Figure 2 (a) Girl worshipping Kṛishna's footprint at Vrindavan. (Bury Peerless.)

Figure 2 (b) Schoolboy praying to Hanuman in a village in Maharahtra. (Bury Peerless.)

was no doubt to do with the tradition itself, the *tat tvam asi* (see above, §2.1). There was warrant in the revelatory texts. But another reason was related to the feeling which also, no doubt, animated Nāgārjuna. It was to do with gnosis, the jñāna or knowledge which we have already encountered in the commentary on the Gītā (Unit 3, §§4.1–4.12). Before going into this second reason for Śaṅkara's strict non-dualism, let us contemplate the concepts of vidyā (which has an important relation to jñāna) and its opposite, *avidyā* or ignorance. For the problem of liberation is also the question of what we need liberation from. And for Śaṅkara that is avidyā, which is not merely lack of knowledge, but defective knowledge, arising from misconceived thinking.

Bottom Page 5 + 9

avidya. Lack of knowledge defective knowledge misconceived thinking

2.4.2 This ignorance or avidyā is the root cause of trouble, as original sin is for the Christian tradition, and its basic form is failure to recognize the sole reality of Brahman. Thus taking the world as real and as something other than the unique Holy Power is ignorance; as from an inner point of view the sense of being an individual also is. From the outer end, the acceptance of the cosmos as other than Brahman, and from the inner point of view the acceptance of individuality as other than the ātman, are two sides of the coin of ignorance. From the standpoint of the lower, everyday truth, this ignorance means being bound to the cycle of rebirth, but more positively it can involve acceptance of śruti and the worship of the Lord—such works and aspirations being in effect a kind of preparation for the higher life which should culminate in true knowledge, vidyā or jñāna. This brings liberation—which looked at from the lower level is release from rebirth, and from the higher level is simply the realization of identity with the Absolute.

2.4.3 So then for Advaita liberation is not brought about by God's grace. The religion of worship is not the highest kind. What achieves salvation is a higher knowledge formed in mystical experience. Thus the general value-system of Advaita is like that of the Mahāyāna. (Further reference will be made to this in your study of Buddhism in Units 5–7.) In Mahāyāna Buddhism, despite the fact that there are celestial Buddhas for worship, in the last resort it is the experience of the ultimate, the Void, which counts, and this fits into the yogic tradition of India. This is reflected by the theory of two levels—the higher truth is to do with ineffable mystical gnosis, while the lower level among other things relates to God and the religion of bhakti and the practice of Vedic ritual. As we shall see, this was a main reason for Rāmānuja's criticism of Advaita. But at least Śaṅkara managed a remarkable synthesis and ordering of religious and ritual ideals.

2.5 Śaṅkara's cosmology

2.5.1 However, there remain some problems about how Śaṅkara conceived of Brahman and ātman. For instance he assigned knowledge of Brahman to the higher level, and about that nothing was to be said discursively: yet on the other hand he used elements in the Upanishadic thinking later expressed in the celebrated formula concerning the Divine, viz. that is *saccidānanda* (i.e. *sat, cit* and *ānanda*). These three terms mean 'being', 'consciousness' and 'bliss' respectively. Sat, incidentally, is the neuter of an adjective of which the feminine is *satī*, a good woman—hence the English term 'suttee', for the good woman is the one who burns herself on her husband's funeral pyre. Thus though sat means, primarily, 'being', there is also a connotation of goodness. This is not a coincidence, but arises from the fact that in religion as elsewhere terms such as 'real' imply value, as when we talk of a real friend, or a real bargain. Hence in the Christian tradition some theologians referred to God as the *ens realissimum* or most real being: the use of the superlative indicates that degrees of reality are being thought of, as if in a scale of excellence, God being the most excellent of all entities. Rudolf Otto in his interesting study *Mysticism East and West*[1] which compares the thought of Śaṅkara and Meister Eckhart, the German mystic, brings out the holy quality of the notion of being.

2.5.2 First, then, Brahman is being. Thus it is possible to know the divine, and it is not a blank. Second, it is cit or consciousness, that is pure undifferentiated consciousness, which is the nature of ātman. Third, Brahman is bliss, because realization of Brahman is the supreme joy and the condition of being liberated or saved. It is like waking up, and leaving behind the perplexities of the dream world. However, it is not possible to

[1] Otto, R. (1932) *Mysticism East and West* (trans. Lacey, B. and Payne, R.) Macmillan.

particularize further concerning Brahman's nature, but one detects in the three inner qualities that constitute the divine essence three aspects of mystical experience; for first such experience of being is like knowing—it is a gnosis,[1] and so one is as it were in contact with the real. Secondly, it is pure consciousness from which all wordly images and discursive thoughts have been banished; and thirdly in its liberating and liberated sense of wholeness it is bliss. But all this of course is applicable at the higher level of truth. Brahman had also, as we have seen, a lower aspect. Śaṅkara thus distinguishes between Brahman *nirguṇam* and *saguṇam*, i.e. Brahman without qualities (*guṇas*) and Brahman with guṇas.

2.5.3 At the lower level Brahman appears as personal Creator. He is Iśvara, and is typically symbolized as either *Śiva* or *Vishṇu*, although he is also known as *Brahmā*, the masculine version of the neuter term Brahman. As Creator he attracts devotion and worship. This notion of levels of divinity was elaborated in later Hinduism, so that different forms under which the divine worshipped correspond to different grades of insight. Thus a late writing states:

> The vulgar look for their gods in water, men of greater insight seek them in heavenly bodies, the ignorant see them in wood and stone, while the wise person sees the Supreme in his own self.

The theory helped to hold together the Hindu synthesis in which all gods, however crude their representation, could be seen as representations of the One. Such a theory also enabled modern Hindus to work out a synthesis, based on Vedānta, between the various religions—Allah, Christ and so forth being so many different fragmentary revelations of the divine Reality.

2.5.4 At the lower level of truth, Śaṅkara's cosmology was conventional. God creates and recreates the cosmos through the usual immense series of *kalpas*, and individuals are seen as implicated in the round of rebirth. However, since strictly there is only one ātman, Śaṅkara's rebirth theory bears a marked resemblance to that of the Buddhists, for as far as the individual goes no separate *purusha* or eternal soul passes over from one life to the next. (You may refer to *Encyclopedia*, pp. 282–284, for further information on the Buddhist teaching.) Apart from the Buddhists and Śaṅkara's Advaita, all other Indian schools which hold the doctrine of rebirth postulate individual souls as the continuing identity of the transmigrating living being. The sense of individuality is indeed that which holds a person to the round of rebirth, and it is to free oneself from that that one should aspire to the higher knowledge.

2.5.5 How then are we to understand the idea that somehow the one Self resides in each one of us? One analogy used is with thinking it to be broken up into portions (e.g. the space within particular jars). The pot, as container, gives the appearance of delimiting a particular space in such a way that it is separated from space itself. Likewise all physical characteristics and our egos are limitations as it were upon the one ātman.

2.5.6 This relationship can be illustrated in the following way. Imagine a box with a light bulb inside it. It has round holes at one end (see Fig. 3). The light streams through the various holes. Looked at from the outside, the box might be said to display a plurality of individual lights; but there is just one source of light, looked at from the inside.

[1] See Unit 3, §4.9.

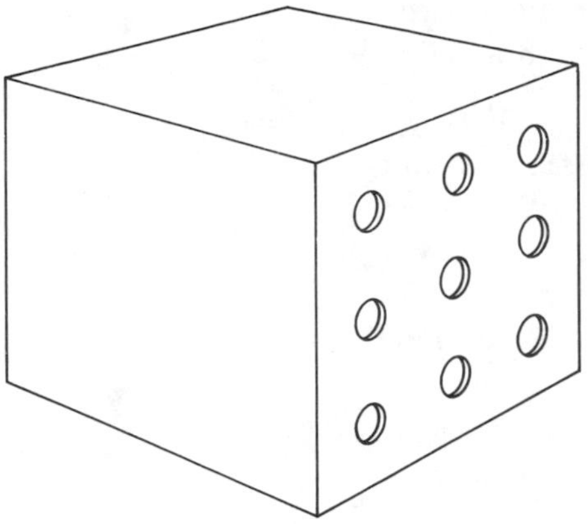

Figure 3

2.5.7 The inability to see the oneness of the divine Self is ignorance, avidyā, which is the psychological counterpart to māyā, the illusion seen as emanating from God (see §2.2.3 above). But how can this ignorance be explained? How is it that we came to project a false multiplicity on to Brahman? How indeed did the whole grand illusion arise? For Śaṅkara these questions are unanswerable. There is a most important sense in which the existence of the illusion is simply inexplicable. Why? Because if one were to give an explanation in terms either of some prior cause or in terms of the purposes or desires of God one would be postulating an explanation which of its nature lies inside the very illusion that we are wishing to explain. So we cannot get beyond the fact of the illusion, a fact however which can only truly be shown by the higher experience of the unity of Brahman and ātman.

2.5.8 Here we encounter another likeness with Buddhism. For the ultimate vidyā which we may gain and which brings release from rebirth also means the loss of our empirical individuality. No separate soul exists in heaven or beyond. It is simply that a certain sequence will not continue through *samsāra*—for example the Śaṅkara sequence if Śaṅkara is to believed, has finished (on the meaning of saṁsāra see *Encyclopedia*, p. 221). Thus *moksha* or liberation (cf. Unit 3, §1.5) in Advaita is similar in its ineffably mysterious disappearance of the individual to the state of final *nirvāṇa* in Buddhism, which means, as you will see from your study of Buddhism, Units 5–7, the relinquishing of continual rebirth.

Exercise

Attempt a brief summary of the main points in Śaṅkara's cosmology. (You will find additional information for an answer in *Encyclopedia*, pp. 233–234.)

PLEASE PAUSE HERE

DO NOT READ ON UNTIL YOU HAVE COMPLETED THE EXERCISE

Specimen answer

The main points I would include in the summary are: Śaṅkara's view of Reality as being one and indivisible, that only the Absolute is real; that the world was created from a divine personality and has evolved from an interminable series of cycles it has passed through; yet the Absolute—who alone is real—is beyond ordinary description, is without qualities or consciousness, is inseparable, is unlimited and without action. This impersonal Absolute is equated with Brahman, it permeates the whole universe and corresponds to ātman. The true self within is identical with the one reality, but the full identification is realized only through ascetic practice, contemplation and meditation.

It is māyā (illusion) that makes the one Absolute reality appear in various forms, that separates the monism into independent entities. Māyā is the cause of all worthless striving and futile endeavour; the world, once one attains the higher level of absolute truth, is seen as a figment of imagination, is little different from a dream, an illusion. Only the supreme experience of the union of Brahman and ātman can induce the quality of real being and, therefore, of liberation.

2.5.9 Altogether Śaṅkara's theology had an elegance and vitality to it which gave Advaita lasting influence. First, it gave a striking, even stark, account of the great identity utterances of the Upanishads. Second, it gave a neat and fruitful means of reconciling apparent contradictions in *śruti*. Third, it gave a consistent account of the meaning of the Brahma Sūtra. Fourth, it made the mystical experience central and gave pride of place therefore to the yogic quest. Fifth, it maintained the framework of Brāhmaṇical orthodoxy (despite the criticisms of his crypto-Buddhism). Sixth, Śaṅkara gave a vital, though subordinate, place to the *bhakti* religion which from before the time of the Gītā had proved of growing influence among the Indian masses. Seventh, the sophistication of his arguments gave the system of Advaita a powerful intellectual as well as a powerful spiritual status in the continuing debates of Indian philosophy. Finally, Advaita gave new content to older conceptions such as māyā, moksha and Īśvara which enabled Hindus radically to meet with criticism in succeeding centuries. To understand why we need to look at religious developments, especially in South India.

3 Rāmānuja and the knowledge of God

3.1 South Indian theism

3.1.1 There was a strong upsurge, from about the seventh century CE onwards, and notably in southern Dravidian speaking areas, of devotional hymnwriting, which stands as a record of the rigour of bhakti in South India. (For a parallel see *Encyclopedia*, p. 234.) Such devotionalism also became important in other parts of India. It is possible that Śiva had special connections with the Dravidian South, in that it may have been archaic predecessors of medieval Dravidians who populated the Indus Valley Civilization (but linguistic evidence of this remains controversial, as the Indus Valley script remains undeciphered, or if deciphered, only speculatively) and there is some evidence of a Śiva figure in that culture. At any rate, those who worshipped Śiva in the south produced a group of fine hymnodists, known as *nāyanārs*. Also in the same period followers of Vishṇu gave birth to the hymns of the poets known as *ālvārs*.

3.1.2 It was out of this matrix that some of the greatest theistic thought of India was born. Though Vishṇu and Śiva could remain enemies, there was also a movement towards reconciliation, and those who worshipped or recognized both as symbols of the Highest were known as *smārtas*. Thus South Indian theism took three main forms, one *Śaiva* (or the worship of Śivā), one *Vaishṇava* (or the worship of *Vishṇu*) and one which combined the two. As it happened, it was the Vaishṇava tradition which was to make the biggest impact in terms of orthodox doctrine. The Śaiva tradition hived off its own school, known as *Śaiva Siddhānta*, which lies outside the Vedāntic tradition and indeed outside the traditional classification of the six schools of Hindu philosophy to which we have already referred (Unit 3, §4.2.3). In principle, however, its position is close to that of Madhva (see §4 below) in stressing a dualism between God and souls, and between souls and the world. It looked to God as creator and saviour. This school still retains quite a strong influence in Tamil Nadu and in northern Sri Lanka among the Tamil population.

3.1.3 The bhakti movement in South India was potentially a threat to Brāhmaṇ orthodoxy, in that it flourished among the indigenous, non-Brāhmaṇ population. The Sanskritization of South Indian culture was a late event, and the *varṇa* or class structure of North India (cf. Unit 1B, §2.3.4) was not embedded there, so that a division of the population between Aryan Brāhmaṇ and Dravidian masses was evident. However, the Brāhmaṇ class succeeded in taking up themes supplied in the growing religious fervour of the south, and ultimately the work of the ālvārs could be seen within the mosaic of orthodox piety. It was in this context that the writings of Śaṅkara's great critic Rāmānuja, are to be seen. He provided a bridge between the Tamil scriptures and the Veda. (For further information on Rāmānuja, refer to *Encyclopedia*, p. 234.)

3.1.4 One cause of dissatisfaction with Śaṅkara's non-dualism was that it relegated firmly to second place the religion of worship and devotion. As we have seen, God as personal Lord is ultimately part of the great illusion. Yet the dominant motif in South Indian religion at its most fervent was a strong devotionalism. But the worship of God requires a distinction between the worshipper and the focus of worship. The logic of Advaita appears to be that in worshipping the Lord one is in fact worshipping oneself. This indeed

(a)

(b)

Figure 4 These two illustrations show examples of ten of the magnificent carvings in a rock-cut temple dedicated to Śiva, on the island of Elephanta in Bombay harbour. The temple's precise date is unknown, but it probably dates from around the ninth century CE. *It is the last great example of architectural sculpture in Western India. (a) shows the three aspects of Śiva's nature. To the left the skull-crowned head represents his destructive nature. To the right the beautiful face of his wife, the creative principle; in the centre the supreme form of the impassive Śiva Mahadeva (Archaelogical Survey of India.) (b) illustrates the classic pose of Śiva Nataraja, Śiva performing his cosmic dance watched by the gods and the heavenly beings. (John Hinnells).*

remains till today a major point of criticism of non-dualism from the perspective of theistic religion. (This, however, is not to say who is right and who is wrong: the issue of the truth of the different systems is one which we are not handling here.) Further Śaṅkara's exegesis of the scriptures, though brilliant and consistent, did not altogether match the feel of some of them, and notably the Gītā, which seemed much more to lean to theism than to non-dualism. As we have noted, there were grounds to look on the Brahma Sūtra as teaching a form of bhedābheda, or identity-in-difference (cf. §1.1.5 above). Though hard to make sense of or to present with consistency, such a doctrine was different from Advaita, partly because it attempted to give equal weight to both sides of the metaphysical coin, while Advaita relegated the aspect of difference to secondary place. It was indeed hard to believe that the ancient texts meant by māyā what Śaṅkara read into the term. Also, there could be dissatisfaction, at the more dispassionate philosophical level, with a doctrine which created scepticism about everyday knowledge. There was perhaps inconsistency, in any case, in using conventional methods of argument and commentary to undermine conventional knowledge.

3.1.5 For these and other reasons, Advaita was open to criticism. But above all it seemed to Rāmānuja and to others to be destructive of the true theism. And yet, as I have already pointed out (§2.2.1 above) Śaṅkara did not quite see himself in this light, and there are some modern commentators who interpret him in a way compatible with theism: for instance, the gap between the empirical ego and the Self can express the distance between God and humanity sensed in the act of worship, while the lack of definition of Brahman and of salvation can be seen as another instance of that *via negativa* (or negative way) of describing God which has been adopted often by the greatest saints and thinkers in the theistic traditions. Still, at face value, and as interpreted by his followers, Śaṅkara did seem inimical to the kind of theism which was so strong in the South Indian tradition from the seventh century onwards through the next five centuries and more.

inimical – unfriendly hostile unfavourable

3.1.6 Perhaps something of the flavour of that theism can be sensed from a dispute which was to be important among rival groups of those who followed after Rāmānuja. It concerned the nature of the operation of God's grace in the quest for salvation. The two schools called themselves respectively the cat-principle school and the monkey-principle school (see also *Encyclopedia*, p. 237) and did so for the following reason. When a mother cat wishes to transport its kitten from one place to another it picks it up by the scruff of the neck. On the other hand, the mother monkey takes her little one on her hip, but the little monkey has to cling to her as it is transported from here to there. The analogy is with the individual, God and salvation. According to the cat-principle, God transports the soul from here to salvation, and the individual does nothing. Or to put it another way, it is solely by God's grace (*prasāda*) that one is saved. According, on the other hand, to the monkey-principle, the soul must do something (i.e. cling) in order safely to arrive at salvation, though of course it is mainly by God's action that one is saved. These contrasting theories of grace are reminiscent of those which have animated Christian debate from Augustine and Pelagius onwards. At any rate they give a sense of how powerful, even according to the monkey-principle school, is the feeling of dependence upon the Lord in the tradition of Viśishtādvaita and more broadly of South Indian theism.

prasada – God's grace

Visishtadvaita – doctrine developed by Ramanuja – a qualified non-dualistic view of the universe both – vital difference between god – and the world and souls

3.1.7 It may be asked: But how do such ideas of salvation square with the pervasive doctrine of *karma* and rebirth? The answer is a simple, but effective one, namely that karma itself is an expression of God's will, so that if he chooses to save you he will already have caused you to be in the relevant karmic situation. The Śaiva Siddhānta went further and argued that not only is God's saving activity compatible with the theory of karma but it is actually entailed by it. For karma presupposes the apportionment of situations in life to people on the basis of their moral acts in this and previous lives. But this implies a knowledge, indeed a perfect knowledge of the moral law and the virtues and intentions of individuals. Only God could have such knowledge. So karma presupposes God.

3.2 The importance of grace

3.2.1 It may be as well to pause here to consider the question of why grace plays so important a part in so many phases of theistic religion—with Paul, in Islam, in theistic Hinduism, in the Reformation, etc. One way of looking at it is as follows, and here I go back in part to the theory of the holy and numinous of Rudolph Otto, briefly outlined in Unit 3, §4.10. For the person who believes in a supreme and awe-inspiring God, then the gap between God and humanity is immense, indeed infinite. Further God possesses the highest value, and is pictured as beyond death, blissful and so on, and having supreme joys not consistently present for people in their struggling and difficult earthly situation.

3.2.2 It is natural to derive two conclusions from this structure of religious belief. The first is that one can achieve nothing in comparison with and in relation to God, unless God facilitates it. Second, salvation is becoming like God, but only God can, so to say, give of his own good things and share deathlessness and beatitude with us. Consequently if there is salvation it is through the action of God, and in general this means the operation of his grace. It is through that grace that I become like him, even in the most shadowy way. In brief, there is a logic running from the numinous experience through to the idea of grace. But there is an *if* in the argument, as I have outlined it. That concerns the question of whether in fact God wishes to share, whether he loves us. The consensus of theism is that people indeed experience that love; and that in any case his action as creator indicates a desire to expand his goodness. Thus paradoxically the awesome, frightening God is also tender and compassionate. There are reasons for the two aspects in his nature, as seen through the religious experience, to go together. If God is also seen in myth as capricious and even roguish, this is partly to express the notion that his goodness is not to be taken for granted: his grace really is a gift, not simply an inevitable consequence of his nature. It is inevitable that he bestows grace, for God is love, but inevitable, in a sense, that it should not be inevitable, for he is God. Is that contradictory? Maybe, for doctrines of grace, natural religious experience, have plenty of theological problems in the differing traditions. That is one reason why the cats scrap with the monkeys in South India, after the time of Rāmānuja.

3.2.3 If an emphasis on grace was central to Rāmānuja's theology, what else followed? It is clear that there must be a powerful doctrine of the created dependence of the world upon God. For if karma is an expression of his will, and if karma's operations cannot (as they cannot) be disentangled from the whole material and spiritual working of the universe, then the ongoing events of the cosmos must depend on God's will. Thus bhakti religion did not just dictate some view of grace as necessary to salvation; it also required a doctrine of God's domination over the central world. Thus bhakti demanded a radical theism. But Rāmānuja formulated that theism under some major restrictions, and in an unexpected way—at least a way unexpected for the Westerner, used to a different style of monotheism.

3.3 Rāmānuja's cosmology

3.3.1 When considering Rāmānuja's cosmology and theism you must remember that like Śaṅkara he was an orthodox *Brāhmaṇ* who believed in the authoritativeness of the Vedic scriptures and in the inspiration of the Gītā. So he needed to be a commentator as well as an exponent of his own insight. It would be false to suppose he wanted to get away from

Figure 5 Śiva and his consort Umā. Bronze, Chola style, about 1000 CE. *(Crown copyright. Victoria and Albert Museum.)*

Figure 6 Children by a small Śiva lingam, South India. (Bury Peerless.)

Figure 7 Śiva in all forms (viṣhvarupa) dancing. (Bhaktapur Museum, Bhaktapur, Photatelier H. Thiele and H. Munker.)

Brāmaṇical traditions—just that he wished to see them in the light of the powerful bhakti tradition to which as a South Indian he was heir. So Rāmānuja's theology follows a similar style to that of Śaṅkara—he wrote important works on the Brahma Sūtra and on the Gītā,[1] for example. If he drew on Tamil sources, he wrote in Sanskrit, the holy language of the great Hindu tradition. Further, he stayed rather faithful to the identity-in-difference theory apparently expressed by Bādarāyaṇa.[2] It was his way of doing this which makes his doctrine of God's control over the world rather unexpected, as I have indicated.

bhedabhedavada

[1] Unit 3, §4.
[2] In the first century CE.

3.3.2 The main feature of his doctrine of the dependence of the world on God was his theory that the cosmos, and also the souls implicated in it, are God's body. So God from one point of view stands to the world as the soul stands to the body. It must be remembered of course that the soul–body relationship in the Indian tradition tends to be treated differently from the way it is in the main Western tradition. Now at first sight such a theory might seem to contradict the claim that God is really independent of the cosmos. After all, it might be argued that I am greatly a creature of my body: its chemistry may determine my moods, while if I am to go anywhere my body must be transported by train, car or whatever. So at first sight it hardly seems a promising doctrine to go with the bhakti demand for a sense of the absolute dependence of the world upon the Lord. This is where Rāmānuja's originality becomes apparent, for he used an analysis of the body in the service of his theology. For him, a body is in principle the instrument of the soul. But with finite beings, and in particular humans, the body, though instrumental to the soul, is imperfectly in its control. For example, though I can raise my hand, normally, at will, I cannot easily control my rate of heartbeat or the way my kidneys function. So though some of my bodily functions seem greatly under my control others are minimally so. So much for finite beings. But the Lord is of course totally in control of his body. So it is totally instrumental to his purposes.

3.3.3 This conception made the idea of identity-in-difference intelligible. There is a sense in which the world is one with God, for it is his body: just as I might say that someone brushed against me, for he brushed against my body, so one can up to a point identify God's body with God. Yet he also transcends his body, so from another point of view he is different from the cosmos. By such an analogy Rāmānuja gave a rationale to the apparent message of the Brahma Sūtra and also those many sacred texts which spoke of the material world, prakṛiti, as somehow an aspect of God's being. The universe was a modification of his substance, or a way in which he in part had evolved. For Rāmānuja was faithful to that theory of causation to which we have referred earlier, namely the *satkāryavāda*, whereby the effect is another form of the cause. For example, when milk turns into curds, the cause (milk) and the effect (curds) are identical. Such a model was applied to all change, so that the events we observe are in effect transformations of an underlying substance.

3.3.4 But though sometimes he has been seen in the West, together with other Hindu thinkers, as a pantheist, such a judgment rests upon a misunderstanding, for several reasons. First, it was, to put no fine point on it, not a spiritual error, though it could of course be a philosophical one, to espouse the theory of satkāryavāda rather than its main rival, the non-identity theory (i.e. the non-identity between cause and effect—a theory held by the Buddhists and by the *Vaiśeshika* school) (see Unit 3, §4.2). Second, Rāmānuja did not strictly wish to identify the material world with God. God always transcends the material manifestation. Third, his strong expousal of bhakti and powerful criticism of monism are evidence of his essentially theistic stance. But of course the style of thought in Rāmānuja is very different from that in the Western monotheistic tradition. (Also, of course, the style of his actual piety differed, for the Hindu gods have a very different symbolism from the God of the Semitic traditions such as Judaism and Islam.)

3.3.5 Since the world is totally dependent for its functioning on the purposes of God, it follows that karma is, as already indicated, an expression of his will. However, what about souls? They are the third angle of the God–world–soul triangle of Indian theology and philosophy. Here again Rāmānuja uses the soul–body analogy, save that now self (for instance) is seen as containing within it a soul, or if you like a soul within the soul, known as the *antaryāmin*, or 'inner controller'.

3.3.6 This last doctrine had a number of advantages. First it made sense of those passages in the Upanishads and elsewhere which spoke of the Divine as within the heart, tinier than a mustard-seed etc. To revert to the language of the Īśā Upanishad, as Self of the cosmos God is far; as Self within the self he is near. Second, this idea of a divine inner controller made sense of the operation of grace in guiding the individual to liberation. Third, it preserved a symmetry in the soul–body analogy between God's relation to the world and his relation to individual selves. It also, for Rāmānuja, provided the key to the interpretation of the mahāvākya, the *tat tvam asi*, which he sees as meaning that God is the self within self, not that God and the individual self are identical. All this re-emphasizes the dependence of the world, both as nature and as karma, upon the action of God.

3.3.7 As we have seen, the idea of God's transformation into the manifest world is a way of stressing God's complete creative control. There is a formal analogy with the Christian conception of creation out of nothing, *ex nihilo*. For in both the Christian doctrine and that of Viśishtādvaita (see §1.1.3 above) God does not depend on anything outside himself as material from which he fashions the world. (Here there is a contrast with such views as those of Plato in the *Timaeus* and elsewhere, where the World-Designer or Demiurge has to make use of somewhat recalcitrant matter—it is that which he shapes into the world we know and which accounts for its partial unintelligibility and evil nature.) However, unlike most of the Christian tradition, Rāmānuja does not consider the universe in principle as having a beginning; it is continuously being created, collapsed into latency and recreated. Thus in effect there is here an idea of continuous creation.

3.4 Salvation and revelation

3.4.1 The strong emphasis upon human dependence might lead to a certain lack of moral concern. After all, if salvation lies wholly in the power of the Lord I do not need to do anything about it. Such a thought is not absent from other systems of belief, such as Calvinism, which have assigned the salvation of men to God's action alone. However, God is loving, and hence the devotion which he instils into his worshippers is also loving. In other words, good actions flow from faith. To be more precise, the devotee should display the following characteristics: goodwill to all creatures, absence of ill-will, faith in the Lord's protection, resort to the Lord as saviour, and a sense of helplessness before him. So the devotee necessarily, out of his good will, becomes a co-worker with God in the process of salvation, and so looks ultimately to the salvation of all people.

3.4.2 In the case of Rāmānuja that salvation means something very different from the liberation referred to in Advaita. The latter involves, as we saw, the complete loss of individual identity. From at least two points of view this seemed wrong to Rāmānuja. First, all consciousness involves a subject–object relationship; so that the liberated soul has a relationship to something else (viz. God). Thus its happiness is conceived as its consciousness of God in a purified state in which the soul shows its affinity to the divine nature.

3.4.3 Second, the relationship of love and adoration implies the cherishing by God of the individual. From one point of view the individual soul is an offshoot from the divine essence, but it has its separate existence and worth. So the mere merging of the self in God and in effect its disappearance was not an attractive idea of liberation, but more like destruction. As for the creature in the saved state—the liberated souls are pictured as in the heavenly realm of Vishṇu, *Vaikuṇṭha*, where they live eternally in glorious proximity to the divine Being.

3.4.4 This whole scheme of belief is derived from *śruti* and *smṛiti* (see Unit 3, §1.3). Rāmānuja of course, makes use of philosophical arguments about the nature of knowledge, for instance, in order to refute his Advaitin opponents, and to interpret the scriptural revelation. But he does not consider that men can have independent knowledge of God, outside the revelations accorded by God himself. In this he is like a number of modern Christian theologians, notably Karl Barth (b. 1886) who thought that traditional Roman Catholic and other claims that there is a natural as well as a revealed knowledge of God involved some contradiction with the doctrine of grace and of salvation by faith alone.[1] For knowledge of God is knowledge for salvation: and if I can get such knowledge on my own, by reasoning, then my salvation is partly my own work, not God's. (Of course it could be argued that reason itself is God given and God-inspired.) In any event, Rāmānuja argued vigorously against the main supposed proofs of God's existence current in the Indian tradition of his day. It is worth exploring these arguments briefly, for in some degree they indicate some vital themes in Indian religious philosophy.

3.4.5 The main arguments for God's existence had been set forth in a work of the *Nyāya-Vaiśeshika* school by Udayana (c. 1000 CE), called the *Kusumañjali* (see *Encyclopedia*, p. 231). The chief arguments had to do with the apparent design of the universe. Thus since the cosmos is a complex whole, made up of parts, it needs a designer (just as we observe complex objects, artifacts, which have been put together by a craftsman). Also the universe bears a resemblance to a living organism, and this presupposes an underlying soul. By such inferences, it was thought, God's existence could be established—though the thought that this was so was not to the liking of everyone. Thus from a position almost diametrically opposite to Rāmānuja's, the *Mīmāṃsā* school of exegesis postulated the intrinsic authoritativeness of the Vedic scriptures (see Unit 3, §4.2). They thus considered them everlasting for if they had been brought into existence (e.g. by a God), then their authority would not be intrinsic but would derive from him. Thus in the name of scriptural orthodoxy they derived the existence of an Iśvara, and even saw the Vedic gods as merely names used in certain ritual acts. Indeed they interpreted the scriptures as nothing but a series of injunctions concerning rites, and not as involving statements of doctrine at all. Thus they were in the rather extraordinary position of combining atheism with a high regard for ritual.

3.4.6 However, the objections of the Viśishtādvaita to Indian natural theology (i.e. knowledge of God based on the exercise of natural reason) proved more vital. In his great commentary on the Brahma Sūtra Rāmānuja outlined among others, the following counter-objections to the argument from design. First, though we have experience of how artifacts are made we have no experience of the origin of the cosmos and so cannot infer

[1] These doctrines were expounded in Barth's massive *Commentary on Romans*, published in 1919.

a like cause. Even, second, if we could it would not follow that there is t one god—like a palace the world might be made by many agents. ird, there could be separate creations in any case for the different world cycles. Fourth, human artifacts work through a body: by inference God should too—but then what created the body through which he fashions the world? That would need another body and so on *ad infinitum*. Again, the resemblance of the universe to an organic being requiring a soul is not close. Mountains for example, do not breathe.

3.4.7 Worse than all these objections is the following one, worse that is from the point of view of the religious worshipper. The stronger the resemblance between the world and an artifact, the stronger the inferred resemblance between God and a human artificer. But the stronger the resemblance the stronger the argument. Thus the stronger the argument, the more anthropomorphic God is. So if God is to be truly exalted and different from mere humans then the argument to his existence is bound to be weak anyway. Thus are the defenders of natural theology impaled on a dilemma. (Incidentally, some of Rāmānuja's arguments here were evolved independently in the *Dialogue on Natural Religion* of the eighteenth-century Scottish philosopher David Hume, which is a critique of the argument from design.)[1]

3.4.8 As we have seen, Rāmānuja's motive was to protect the sovereignty of God and the authoritativeness of the revelations which he gave to the ṛishi or seers of old. Thus his theory of how we know about God is of a piece with the whole of his bhakti theology.

Exercise

From what you have read about Śaṅkara and Rāmānuja, write your own summary of their views on moksha or liberation. (Refer to the relevant material in *Encyclopedia*, pp. 233–235.)

PLEASE PAUSE HERE

DO NOT READ ON UNTIL YOU HAVE COMPLETED THE EXERCISE

Specimen answer

Śaṅkara concentrates upon knowledge as the key to liberation. If you truly know the distinction between the eternal and the impermanent—that is, between the real and the unreal—then you realize one's true status (namely identity with Brahman). In order to achieve such knowledge, you need to transcend the religion of worship and ritual, so that it is ultimately no good praying or relying upon the usual procedures of ordinary religion.

On the other hand Rāmānuja fervently stresses devotion (bhakti) and the operation of God's grace. One main objection he had to Advaita was that the idea of illusion (māyā) extended to God's activity, in other words God's salvation would be illusory if Śaṅkara were right. So Rāmānuja stresses the reality of the Divine Being; and this being so liberation must stem from God. So for Rāmānuja liberation comes from above, and for Śaṅkara it comes from within.

[1] David Hume (1711–1776) made his critique in his *Philosophical Essays Concerning Human Understanding*, London 1748, later published as *An Inquiry Concerning Human Understanding*, London, 1861.

Or to put these matters another way: for Advaita the person is truly the Divine Being. The only obstacle to liberation is ignorance of one's true status. For Viśishtādvaita the person is dependent on God, not on the Self.

3.4.9 One last point may be made about Rāmānuja's theism which is also relevant to that of Madhva, to which we shall turn shortly. As noted already, the *Sāṇkhya* scheme of guṇas and theory of evolution in a pulsating cosmos was used in Vedānta and more widely in the explanation of creation in Vaishṇava theology. But it also happened that the doctrine of a plurality of souls (virtually an infinite number) scattered through prakṛiti and involved in saṁsāra was more consonant with theism than with Śaṅkara's monism (see above, §2.5). For if the soul and God are separate (the theistic view) then it more or less inevitably follows that there are many souls. Thus Sāṅkhya though atheistic could be given a theistic application.

4 Madhva and personal particularity

4.1 The influence of Jainism and Christianity

4.1.1 If Rāmānuja steered a middle path, with Śaṅkara veering in a monistic direction, then Madhva veered in the opposite, radically dualistic direction (see *Encyclopedia*, pp. 234–235). Perhaps one of the must ironic aspects of his interpretations of the *Upanishads* is his treatment of the saying *sa ātmā tat tvam asi*, usually translated as 'That self; that art thou' (see §1.1.2 above). It is worth noting that classical Sanskrit is normally written continuously and not broken up (as modern Romanized transliterations are) into separate words. Thus in written form the saying in question becomes *sātmātattvamasi*. Now if we consider the part *ātmātat* we get the following consideration.

Suppose it broke up into *ātmā* and *atat* it would still end up *ātmātāt*, for the *a*- of *atat* would get so to say swallowed up in the long *a* of *ātmā*. Vowels elide and coalesce in Sanskrit. So conceivably instead of *tat tvam asi* we should have *atat tvam asi*.

Now in Sanskrit as in Greek (e.g. in Greek derivatives like 'atheist') the prefix *a* means 'non', hence if the hypothesis about *atat* were correct the great saying would mean the contradictory of 'that art thou', namely 'not-that art thou'. By this bold stroke Madhva reversed Advaita! He affirmed the essential difference between self and Brahman. Hence his system is known as Dvaita.

4.1.2 The milieu in which Madhva was brought up in Western India, had been a strong area of *Jainism*, and it may be that he was influenced by the *Jain* belief in the essential difference between souls and non-living matter (see *Encyclopedia*, p. 259, on the subject of this difference). It also happens that the area was one in which Christianity had long been represented (it had been established in South India according to legend by Thomas the Apostle, and certainly was there very early); and some have seen Christian influences upon Madhva (refer to the notice of this influence in *Encyclopedia*, p. 235). Thus he gave a special place to the god *Vāyu*, wind or spirit. Some miracles ascribed to him such as walking on water might indicate Christian influence. And he was the first great Indian theologian to postulate permanent damnation as a possibility for some souls, and this again may have Christian provenance. However, the coincidences can be explained in other ways. But the question of damnation requires some further comment.

4.1.3 The Indian religious imagination was able to conceive some pretty horrid punishments beyond the grave. Buddhism, Jainism and Hinduism all have their scenes of torment. But generally such hells were not true hells—more purgatories, just as most heavens were seen as impermanent. Thus after one had worked off the effects of one's sin (maybe over thousands of millions of years) one would emerge to a better existence. In other words, damnation was not final (see *Reader*, §2.7 'The meaning of *moksha* in contemporary Hindu thought and life'). Nothing was final except moksha. So in general, liberation was the one means of attaining a permanent status. However, there was the notion that some souls would never emerge from rebirth (but this did not entail hellish punishment all or most of the time: a lot of the time could for that matter be heavenly). But the thought of a destiny of perdition was, till Madhva, largely foreign to the Indian tradition.

4.2 The uniqueness of souls

4.2.1 There were different reasons for this idea, leaving aside the question of Christian influence, but they turned essentially upon Madhva's strong sense of the particularity of things and of living beings more specially. Being particular and distinct they should have varying destinies. Madhva was critical of the Advaita concept of a higher non-dualist knowledge (though he had been taught in his young days by a non-dualist guru), since he analysed all knowledge as involving a relationship (i.e. between the knower and the object known; for a further reference to this concept of relationship, see *Encyclopedia*, p. 235). But also, it did not make sense to speak of the object known, or for that matter of the knower, except in terms of an individual entity not some abstraction. Consequently Madhva concluded that all knowledge is not merely dualistic but highly particular. Every particular in the world is different both numerically and in its attributes from every other particular in the world. Thus souls differ from one another, and each one is unique.

Question

What consequences follow for our estimate of the individual from Madhva's teaching on the uniqueness of the soul? (Refer to *Encyclopedia*, pp. 234–235 for additional information.)

PLEASE PAUSE HERE

DO NOT READ ON UNTIL YOU HAVE COMPLETED THE EXERCISE

Specimen answer

A possible answer might be along the following lines.

Any estimate of individual worth and status must take into account the criterion of uniqueness. According to Madhva everything relating to the individual, including knowledge, is unique and particular. This leads to the assumption of a unique individual density. Thus every individual soul is able to draw close to God and contemplate his glory in a relationship of devotion. The individual is the object of God's grace as a special gift to the righteous. In this way Madhva postulated the otherness of God and the existence in him of attributes that none other can possess. His way of dealing with the individual gives respect to the intrinsic worth of each and the particularity of the individual is not blurred even when that person reaches the state of liberation.

4.2.2 In this conception Madhva runs contrary to a trend in traditional Indian thinking (e.g. in Sāṅkhya), which conceived of souls as standardized. There is, that is to say, nothing intrinsic to my soul to differentiate it from yours, beyond the fact that my soul is entangled with my sequence of rebirths and yours with yours. Souls are as alike as peas, but happen to get into different pods. All this, of course, reinforces a tendency to think of liberation not as fulfilling individuality, but actually getting rid of it to the highest degree. The special characteristics which mark off my sequence of rebirths from yours, and my character in this life from yours, simply vanish when I achieve liberation. Moksha might, then, be seen as the self-destruction of the individual personality and sense of identity. But Madhva on the contrary considers that even in liberation differences must remain. It is thus not altogether surprising that he has different permanent forms of being saved or not saved. (Though should he not in strict logic have had an infinite number of categories of final judgment? Perhaps, but we should recall that there will be nuances of difference in each soul's final state, where it has one, because of its own individual characteristics.) It is of course conceivable that in this doctrine of personal particularity, again, Madhva was under Christian influence. However it is hard to measure, since he advanced quite independent arguments for his position, based on his analysis, as we have seen, of the nature of knowledge—and there are some resemblances between his theory here and that of the Jains.

4.3 Determinism and dependency

4.3.1 Now if each individual is different intrinsically from every other, it seems to follow that no two sequences of karma governing rebirth will be alike. Madhva indeed went further than this and saw each individual's inner character unfolding as it were in the operation of karma from life to life. That is somewhat like the Calvinist idea of predestination, save in the Dvaitin case there are millions of successive lives to consider and, for many souls, an infinite number. This gives a deterministic air to Madhva's system, and recalls some early Indian theories that those who are destined for moksha will attain it and those that are not will not. To look at it another way a soul contains the blueprint for its own destiny within it.

4.3.2 On the other hand, it does not follow that the soul brings about its own salvation. Madhva was consistent upon the need for God's grace. However, that grace is accorded unfailingly to those who are virtuous and devoted to Vishṇu. So God's saving activity matches appropriately the unfolding destiny of the good soul (and his damning activity operates similarly, etc.) The salvation to be expected is life in heaven in proximity to and relationship with, God: here again Madhva postulates different grades of closeness to Vishṇu.

4.3.3 Not only is every soul different from every other but every particle in the material world differs from every other—so Madhva sees the world as made up of a very complex mesh of relationships. Though the universe has always existed (again, Madhva uses the now traditional Indian picture of the pulsating cosmos); and although it is made up of an infinite number of particles and souls, each containing intrinsic characteristics which in a sense determine its future, the cosmos is not independent. The agent which causes the various destinies of souls and particles to unfold and interact is God. The major difference then between worldly things and God is that the former depend for their activity on God, but the converse does not apply; God's activity and existence do not depend upon anything else. God is autonomous, while all other beings are dependent or heteronomous.

5 Bhakti theism

5.1 Śāktism

5.1.1 Superficially it might seem that Madhva's doctrines are close to Western theism than the other versions of Vedānta which we have examined. However, it can be argued that Rāmānuja's concept of creation and of the soul–body relationship gives a much stronger picture of the dependence of the world and of souls upon the Creator. The Dvaitin concept of the intrinsic particularity of each soul seems to give it, and by implication everything in the cosmos, a limited independence from God, so that the latter's work mainly consists in causing certain prearranged fates to be fulfilled. And there is in Rāmānuja a more direct doctrine of salvation by bhakti and the grace of God, even if Madhva stands in the same general Vaishṇava tradition. (For a further account of Madhva's view of salvation

Figure 8 Durgā slaying the buffalo, Mahishasura, Hoysala style, late thirteenth century CE*, Mysore. (Crown copyright. Victoria and Albert Museum.)*

by divine grace, see *Encyclopedia*, p. 235. The Vaishṇva views of God, and the later development of this tradition, are also considered in *Encyclopedia*, p. 224.

5.1.2 It will be seen that bhakti theism was mainly oriented towards the cult of Vishṇu and his incarnations, notably *Kṛishṇa* and *Rāma*. Nevertheless, medieval Hinduism already recognized Śiva and Vishṇu as alternative representations of deity and not necessarily as rivals. But in addition the cult of the female counterparts of the male Deity was important, and as such is often known as Śāktism, from the term *śakti*, referring to the female creative energy of God, pictured as the consort of God or as indeed the divine essence (see also *Encyclopedia*, p. 228). Such Śāktism is more powerful and well-developed on the side of Śaiva Hinduism. No doubt it originates from very early fertility religion; but in its more doctrinal form it holds that the female aspect of divinity is the energetic and creative one (in Indian sexual imagery the female is depicted often as the active partner, the male the passive). The most important deity of Śāktism is Śiva's counterpart, represented as *Durgā* or *Kālī*, and also as *Pārvati* or *Umā*. (On this representation, see also *Encyclopedia*, p. 227.) In the former aspect she is fierce and destructive, yet in principle loving to her devotees; under the latter names she is milder. The ferocity of *Kālī* again should not mislead us—it is in part an expression of the numinous character of the deity.

5.2 Influence of Rāmānanda

5.2.1 The bhakti sects founded by Rāmānuja and Madhva, together with others, prepared the way for an even more radical reformation. For the followers of Rāmānuja were controlled by an organization still dominated by the Brāhmaṇ class; and from his teaching order men of the untouchable class were excluded, despite the theoretical egalitarianism of devotional religion. However, in the late fourteenth and early fifteenth centuries CE, a major figure in the tradition, *Rāmānanda*, who migrated to *Varanasi* (Banaras) in North India from the Rāmānuja centre at *Srīrangapatnam* in Kanara (Mysore), founded an egalitarian order of ascetics which broke with many of the ritual regulations of the main sect. He was to exert a strong influence upon later religious history, in that one of his followers was Kabīr, spiritual ancestor of the group known as the Kabīrpanthis. The sikh religion also resulted from this influence.[1]

5.2.2 With Kabīr bhakti religion took a difficult twist. Whereas the tendency of much Indian devotionalism had been to see God in all sorts of forms—as incarnations of Vishṇu, for instance, but even also in one's guru and in great teachers who tended likewise to become deified, Kabīr and Nānak were faced with the phenomenon of Indian Islam. To the Muslim the cult of images was abhorent, while even relatively harmless practices such as pilgrimage were divisive. On the other hand bhakti was congenial to the Islamic temperament and Rāmānanda's egalitarianism chimed in with the Muslim rejection of the caste system. You will find further references to these matters in your study of Islam in Units 14–15. Thus the time was ripe for a new imageless synthesis embracing the ideals of the two religions, and for the development of the Sikh tradition (though the latter was destined to develop its own forms of external differences from the two older faiths).

[1] On Kabir see Units 1B–2, §§4.10 and 4.11. Sikhism will be studied in Units 8–9.

5.3 Vallabha and Caitanya

5.3.1 Two other figures should be mentioned in the development of North Indian bhakti which flourished widely from the time of Rāmānanda onwards, often expressing itself through poetry and other writings composed in the various northern vernacular languages (Punjābi, Hindi, Bangāli and so on). One of these figures, greatly influenced in establishing a devotional movement full of tenderness and emphasizing Kṛishṇa as the beloved lover of the *gopis* (cow girls) and of *Rādha*, was *Vallabha* who flourished in the second half of the sixteenth century CE. (On the development and standpoint of the Vallabha sect, see *Encyclopedia*, p. 238.) He combined a certain sort of non-dualism with a very strong devotional religion, even this-worldly in emphasis. The divine Being transforms himself into the world and sends forth souls out of a spirit of pure *līlā* or sport. If Brahman is sat, cit and ānanda, then souls in the state of suffering and rebirth are sat, and cit, but lack bliss or ānanda, while the material world is real, sat, but lacks the other two properties. But those who see the world as it truly is, the transformation of Brahman, lose their ignorance and attain salvation or bliss. So ultimately the path of bhakti leads to a sense of union with God; and Vallabha makes use of the sexual imagery often used in religion to signify union with the divine.

5.3.2 Another figure was the Bangāli, *Caitanya*, born in 1485, who as a young man exhibited considerable intellectual prowess, especially in logic, but after a pilgrimage to *Bodh Gāyā*, the Buddhist shrine (but also sacred to Vishṇu since the Buddha came to be identified as an incarnation of Vishṇu), he underwent a strong conversion experience, through which he became devoted to Vishṇu and Krishṇa. As a result he evolved a new and fervent teaching. In order that the love of God inherent in the soul, but clouded over by ignorance, should become manifest, the disciple should devote himself to such practices as chanting God's name, hearing and singing his praises, thinking about the playfulness and beautiful nature of Kṛishṇa and indulging in the rituals of worship. The recounting of the name of God by a rosary he also encouraged. It was out of Caitanya's movement that the modern followers of *Hare Kṛishṇa* have emerged, in a Western adaptation of his fervent devotionalism. However, he was also capable of the highest *samādhi* or unified consciousness which he saw as compatible with bhakti, as though the ultimate stage of love were to be merged with the Beloved. In this he retained the worship of Advaita but in a context which made both the world and worship real. The two sides of Brahman were equally vital. In this he is a forerunner of the nineteenth-century Bangāli saint *Sri Rāmakṛishṇa*. (See further *Encyclopedia*, p. 249–250.)

5.3.3 To sum up: in the early medieval period in South India and later in the North there developed a very strong series of devotional movements often relying on the hymns and piety of vernacular writers, though usually interpreted in terms of some form of Vedānta or other system composed in Sanskrit. Typically the unit of gods under one God was stressed, and this received impetus through the whole theory and practice of worship of the *avatārs* or incarnations of Vishṇu, and the cults of gurus and saints. (On the avatārs, see also Unit 3, §5.1.1.) In North India, partly because of contact with Islam, a move to transcend all visual and material images culminated in the religion of Nānak and Sikh gurus. Meanwhile allegiance to female representations of God remaind an important factor, especially in the North East (e.g. in Bangāl).

(a)

Figure 9 (a)–(f) The Temple of Mahalaxshmi, Bombay. Hindu worship typically is not of a congregational nature. It is an individual affair and based on the offering of respect due to a noble or king. This is a sequence showing worshippers at the Mahalaxshmi temple in Bombay. First (a) the worshipper purchases some offering to make to the deity, a garland or some fruit. Booths are to be found near temples selling suitable offerings. Then (b) the worshipper progresses to the temple. Before entering the sacred precinct he or she must remove their shoes which, for a small fee, will be guarded by women sheltering under umbrellas. (c) On entering the precincts the worshipper rings a bell to announce his or her arrival to the gods, then (d) takes the offering through the door to the sanctuary. Despite the openness of intellectual Hinduism, at the popular level it is more restrictive and non-Hindus cannot enter or photograph (not even with telephoto lenses!) the sanctuary itself where priests receive the offerings and decorate the god (or goddess). Any personal donations (e) offered on a solitary basis facing the entrace of the sanctuary. Holy objects in the precinct are often placed in cages, but the faithful draw comfort from touching and so honouring them or simply adoring them in silence. (f) Having thus offered worship the devotee receives blessing from the holy men present at the temple and returns to the outside world. (John Hinnells.)

(b)

(c)

(d)

(e)

(f)

Patterns of liberation

Exercise on the main 'patterns' of liberation

6.1.1 Try now to summarize the main 'patterns' or the types of liberation outlined in the various Hindu doctrinal systems. (For this exercise, revise the material of §2.5 in this unit, and refer also to relevant passages in *Encyclopedia*, pp. 225–226.)

PLEASE PAUSE HERE

DO NOT READ ON UNTIL YOU HAVE COMPLETED THE EXERCISE

Specimen answer

If we look at early Sāṇkhya it involves belief in many souls or purushas. Yoga virtually uses the same scheme, even if the Lord comes in as a rather marginal extra. In these systems, and also in Jainism, liberation is an individual matter, namely a particular soul leaves the round of rebirth and the empirical is no longer reborn. The stress in these systems is on knowledge and yoga; and to some extent austerity or *tapas*. So one pattern is: many souls and rebirth, but consequently upon the heroic practice of self-control one may achieve a disappearance of one's soul from the round of saṁsāra. In principle, *Theravāda Buddhism* presents a like picture, though nothing can be said about individual liberation once nirvāna has supervened. (Theravāda Buddhism will be studied in Units 5–7.) In any event it looks as if a typical context of early yoga was belief in a plurality of souls and lack of interest either in ritual or in devotion to God as relevant to salvation.

6.1.2 Another pattern is presented by the Upanishads and by Advaita (though this is not to say that Advaita is the only or truest interpretation of the Upanishads), namely of a single Being who also somehow resides in the soul. So it may be that there is but one Soul, identical with God. The practice of meditation within the context of yoga will bring about realization of identity, and escape from samsāra. (On the bondage of saṁsāra, see *Reader*, §2.7.3.) This account also gives some place for devotion as a secondary form of religion, which may be a means of the individual's going higher in the round of rebirth and the scale of the spirit, so that he may reach for the higher experience of *tat tvam asi* (see §1.1 above). But still here, as with Sāṇkhya-Yoga, the main mode of liberation is yoga, and contemplation, while on the other hand, in a rather Buddhist way all individuality is lost in the final achievement of moksha.

6.1.3 The third main pattern is found in the Gītā and in the bhakti schools; in this, the plurality of souls is on the whole maintained and yet they are not seen as being liberated into a kind of isolation, as with Yoga, or into an identity with Brahman, as in Advaita—but rather into a kind of communion with the Divine. The means is ultimately God's grace, but looked at from the perspective of this world, it is devotion, which may indeed involve *prapatti* or 'clinging to' God (as according to the monkey-school referred to earlier in §3.1.6). Sometimes in the Gītā and elsewhere it is thought that the yogi who concentrates on identifying with Brahmā becomes Brahmā, but only as a lower aspect of the Lord's nature. In other words, the highest happiness is in a self-conscious heaven where the soul recognizes both God and itself.

6.1.4 Broadly these are the three types of salvation in mainstream Hinduism, and they depend on whether bhakti or meditation is stressed, or both (see Unit 3, §4.2). Or, with one or two schools such as Mīmāmasā, neither: here the concept of heaven as a reward for ritual practice is a return to early thoughts in the Vedic period, long suspended by the belief in rebirth and the different drives of yogi and devotee, with difficulty absorbed and kept in control by Brāhmaṇ orthodoxy.

Also we must not forget that some of these ways to liberation could be seen, as in the Gītā, as allied to the path of action, the *karma mārga*, and so available to ordinary men in the pursuance of their caste and other duties.

6.1.5 The movements outlined above prepared the way for modern Hinduism, where as has been indicated (Unit 3, §4.2), Vedānta could acquire a new life. The present discussion of Indian doctrine has been orientated towards religious ideals, but at the same time many important ideas in Indian philosophy have necessarily been omitted. It is, however, wise to recognize that Indian religious movements have tended to have a strong intellectual dimension, even if basically they stem from fundamental forms of religious experience and practice, such as yoga and bhakti. (Refer again to *Reader*, §§2.7.1–2.7.4.)

6.2 Retrospect on the Hindu quest[1]

Now for a recapitulatory exercise on the Hindu religious quest.

Exercise

6.2.1 Taking the overall theme of the course as set out in Unit 1A, say briefly how the basic doctrines of Hinduism constitute a diagnosis of the human predicament and of the religious quest for liberation. In other words, *from* what are people liberated? *to* what does liberation bring them? and *by* what means are they liberated?

PLEASE PAUSE HERE

DO NOT READ ON UNTIL YOU HAVE COMPLETED THE EXERCISE

Specimen answer and discussion

6.2.2 There is more than one point of view from which to consider Hinduism's concern with the human predicament. We can approach the question in an objective and analytic way, or in a direct and subjective way. The former would allow for a critical examination of the body of Hindu doctrine about deliverance or liberation, the other would be more intuitive and experiential.

6.2.3 The diagnosis of the human predicament must expose the different aspects of Hindu thought, and then attempt to integrate the parts into a

[1] This recapitulatory exercise and answer, including §§6.2.1–6.2.5, has been contributed by Dr. J. G. Harris, to whom Prof Smart and the course team acknowledge their indebtedness for editorial assistance in the preparation of Units 3 and 4.

homogeneous whole. Nevertheless we need not expect to succeed in this attempt, since as we have seen, there are within Hinduism diametrically opposed interpretations of reality. Human life is set against the universe, and it is in this setting that the quest for liberation has meaning. Liberation is the development of the process whereby the individual expresses the ātman within, and the goal is the end of separation, entry upon the higher experience of *tat tvam asi*. The goal is made possible from the beginning by Brahman, the Absolute Reality, who is also the 'holy power' who envelops the universe and whose all-pervasiveness makes possible the union of the ātman (the Self) with Brahman.

6.2.4 The union can be achieved by the renunciation of the world and following the paths of *brahmacārin*, *gṛihasta*, *vanaprastha* and *sannyāsin* (Unit 3, §3). Furthermore, the practice of yoga, and the purification that ensues, as well as the pursuit of knowledge (vidyā), are means to the attainment of the ideal. The process of liberation may be conceived as a divine action in the soul. According to this theistic conception, a person can experience the charismatic aspect of God's nature, wherein, paradoxically, awesomeness and grace exist together. The practice of devotion (Unit 3, §3.1) provides a further means for the attainment of liberation, for hereby is effected reconciliation, which is part of the theistic tradition of Hinduism, and, as Madhva taught, of knowledge attained through relationship, that is, through forging a relationship between the knower and the known.

6.2.5 To sum up, then, for the most part Hinduism sees liberation as *from* a world of dissatisfaction and suffering, in which we are implicated for ever, unless freed, in the ceaseless round of rebirth. Liberation is often seen as *by* Gold's loving action, but often also as by various techniques used by people to overcome the drag of karma. Liberation translates a soul beyond heaven *to* perfect peace or within heaven to the perfectly satisfying communion with God.

6.2.6 But also it is worth reflecting that because of the belief in rebirth the Indian, whether Hindu or other, has more frequently seen his or her future as

Figure 10 Modern Hindu sage, Bombay beach. (John Hinnells.)

open to many alternatives—as animal, ghost, god, criminal in purgatory, higher human, soul liberated. It is a more bewildering, more complex prospect regarding salvation than people have been used to in the West. It is a hierarchy of liberations and entanglements, ranging from purgatories through earth to ranges of heavens and finally the transcendent world. Maybe such a hierarchical society suits a hierarchical universe.

7 Further reading

Basham, A. L. (1954) *The Wonder that was India,* Sidgwick & Jackson, London.

Carpenter, J. Estlin (1921) *Theism in Medieval India,* Williams & Norgate, London.

Daniélou, A. (1964) *Hindu Polytheism,* Routledge & Kegan Paul, London.

Edgerton, F. (1944) *The Bhagavadgītā,* 2 vols., Harvard University Press.

Hiriyanna, M. (1949) *The Essentials of Indian Philosophy,* Allen & Unwin, London

Potter, K. (1973) *The Presuppositions of India's Philosophies,* Greenwood, New York.

Radhakrishnan, S. (1968) *The Principal Upanishads,* Allen & Unwin, London.

Radhakrishnan, S. (1948) *The Bhagavadgītā,* Allen & Unwin, London.

Zaehner, R. C. (1962) *Hinduism,* Oxford University Press.

Zimmer, H. (1957) *The Philosophies of India,* Dewer Books, London.

See the Course Guide for updated further reading.

A228 The Religious Quest

Unit 1A	How to study Religion
Units 1B–2	Hinduism in the Village Setting
Units 3–4	Hindu Patterns of Liberation
Units 5–7	The Noble Path of Buddhism
Units 8–9	The Religion of the Sikhs
Units 10–11	The Religion of the Jews
Units 12–13	The Christian Religion
Units 14–15	Islam and the Muslim